C000264235

VIENNA

TRAVEL GUIDE

2023

All rights reserved. No part of this publication may be reproduced, distributed, or transmitted in any form or by any means, including photocopying, recording or other electronic or mechanical methods, without the prior written permission of the publisher, except in the case of brief quotation embodied in critical reviews and certain other noncommercial uses permitted by copyright law

Copyright by Patrick Seymore 2023

TABLE OF CONTENT

Chapter 1

Introduction

Vienna is a city that is steeped in history, culture, and arts. It is the capital of Austria and one of the most popular tourist destinations in Europe. The city is renowned for its stunning architecture, rich heritage, and vibrant cultural scene. As a visitor, you can immerse yourself in the art and culture of Vienna, explore its museums and galleries, sample its delicious food and wine, and marvel at its beautiful buildings and landmarks.

The purpose of this travel guide is to provide you with all the information you need to plan an unforgettable trip to Vienna in 2023. Whether you are a first-time visitor or a seasoned traveler, this guide will give you an insight into the best things to see and do in the city, as well as practical information on transportation, accommodation, and safety.

Vienna has a fascinating history that dates back over 2000 years. The city has been the home of the Habsburgs, one of Europe's most influential royal families, for over 600 years. During this time, Vienna has been a center of political, cultural, and economic power. The legacy of this rich history is still visible in the city's stunning architecture, from Gothic to Baroque to Art Nouveau.

Vienna is a city that is blessed with a diverse range of attractions, from grand palaces to quaint coffee shops. The city's top tourist attractions include the Schönbrunn Palace, which was the summer residence of the Habsburg emperors; the Hofburg Palace, which was the winter residence of the Habsburgs and now houses several museums; St. Stephen's Cathedral, which is the most important religious building in Vienna; and the Belvedere Palace, which is home to a world-renowned collection of Austrian art.

Vienna is also renowned for its cultural and artistic scene. The city has been the home of many famous artists and musicians, including Mozart, Beethoven, and Klimt. Today, Vienna is home to several world-class museums and galleries, such as the Kunsthistorisches Museum and the Albertina. The city is also famous for its opera, with the Vienna State Opera being one of the most prestigious opera houses in the world.

Vienna is also famous for its culinary delights. The city is home to several traditional Viennese restaurants, where you can sample dishes such as Wiener Schnitzel and Tafelspitz. Vienna is also famous for its coffee culture, with many quaint coffee shops and cafés serving up delicious cakes and pastries.

Finally, Vienna is also an excellent base for day trips to other parts of Austria and neighboring countries such as Slovakia and Hungary. The Wachau Valley, Melk Abbey, Salzburg, and Graz are just a few of the places that you can visit on a day trip from Vienna.

In conclusion, Vienna is a city that has something for everyone. Whether you are interested in history, culture, art, food, or simply want to relax and enjoy the city's vibrant atmosphere, Vienna is a destination that you should not miss in 2023. This travel guide will help you to plan your trip and make the most of your time in this beautiful and fascinating city.

Vienna is not only a city of history and culture but also a city of green spaces. The city has over 280 parks, including the famous Prater Park, which is home to the Riesenrad Ferris wheel and a range of attractions. The city also has several public gardens, such as the Volksgarten and the Burggarten, where you can relax and enjoy the beautiful scenery.

Vienna is also a city that is renowned for its shopping. The city has a diverse range of shops, from designer boutiques to quirky independent stores. The Mariahilfer Strasse is the city's main shopping street, where you can find a range of high street shops and department stores. The Graben and Kohlmarkt are also popular shopping streets, with several luxury boutiques and jewelry stores.

If you are interested in exploring Vienna's artistic scene, then the MuseumsQuartier is a must-visit. This cultural complex is home to several museums and galleries, including the Leopold Museum, which houses a world-renowned collection of Austrian art. The MuseumsQuartier is also home to several bars and restaurants, making it a great place to spend an evening.

Vienna is also a city that is steeped in tradition and customs. It is important to be aware of the city's etiquette and customs, such as tipping etiquette and language use. The local language is German, but many people in Vienna speak English. It is always polite to learn a few basic phrases in German, such as please and thank you.

Overall, Vienna is a city that is full of surprises and delights. It is a city that is steeped in history and culture but is also a vibrant and modern metropolis. Whether you are interested in exploring the city's museums and galleries or sampling its delicious food and wine, Vienna is a destination that is sure to impress. This travel guide will help you to plan your trip and make the most of your time in this beautiful city.

Purpose of the guide

The purpose of this travel guide is to provide visitors with a comprehensive resource for planning their trip to Vienna in 2023. It aims to provide practical information on transportation, accommodation, safety, and activities, as well as an overview of the city's rich history, culture, and attractions.

Planning a trip to a new city can be a daunting task, especially if you are unfamiliar with the language, culture, and customs. This guide aims to make the planning process as easy and stress-free as possible by providing all the essential information you need to know before your trip.

One of the main objectives of this guide is to help visitors get the most out of their time in Vienna. The city is packed with things to see and do, from exploring its museums and galleries to sampling its culinary delights. This guide provides a detailed overview of the city's top attractions, as well as some hidden gems that may not be on your radar.

Additionally, this guide aims to provide visitors with practical information on how to get around the city. Vienna has an excellent public transportation system, including buses, trams, and trains, which makes it easy to get around. This guide provides information on how to use public transportation, as well as options for renting cars or bikes.

Another important objective of this guide is to help visitors find suitable accommodation options. Vienna has a wide range of accommodation options, from luxury hotels to budget-friendly hostels. This guide provides information on the different neighborhoods in the city, as well as recommendations for where to stay based on your preferences and budget.

Safety is also a top priority when traveling, and this guide provides important information on how to stay safe in Vienna. The city is generally considered safe, but it is always wise to take precautions to avoid theft and scams. This guide provides tips on how to keep yourself and your belongings safe while exploring the city.

Finally, this guide aims to provide visitors with an appreciation of Vienna's rich history, culture, and traditions. Vienna has a fascinating history, and it is a city that is steeped in art, music, and literature. This guide provides an overview of the city's cultural scene, as well as information on its customs and etiquette.

In conclusion, the purpose of this guide is to provide visitors with all the information they need to plan an unforgettable trip to Vienna in 2023. Whether you are interested in history, culture, or simply want to explore the city's vibrant atmosphere, this guide will help you to make the most of your time in this beautiful city.

This guide also aims to be a valuable resource for travelers of all types, whether you are a solo traveler, a couple, a family, or a group of friends. It provides information on activities that are suitable for all ages and interests, from cultural attractions to outdoor activities.

Furthermore, this guide is designed to be accessible to everyone, regardless of their level of experience in travel planning. It provides practical information in a clear and concise manner, making it easy to understand and navigate.

Additionally, this guide aims to provide visitors with tips and recommendations from locals and experienced travelers. These insights can help visitors to avoid common mistakes, discover hidden gems, and have a more authentic experience of the city.

Lastly, this guide recognizes that Vienna is a city that is constantly evolving, and new attractions and experiences are constantly emerging. Therefore, it is updated regularly to ensure that the information provided is current and accurate.

In summary, the purpose of this guide is to provide visitors with a comprehensive resource that will help them to plan their trip to Vienna in 2023. It provides practical information on transportation, accommodation, safety, and activities, as well as an overview of the city's rich history, culture, and attractions. It aims to be accessible, informative, and up-to-date, and to help visitors of all types have an unforgettable experience in this beautiful city.

Another important aspect of this guide is its commitment to sustainability and responsible tourism. Vienna is a city that values its natural environment, and visitors can play a role in preserving its beauty for future generations. This guide provides information on eco-friendly activities and accommodations, as well as tips on how to minimize your impact on the environment while traveling.

Moreover, this guide recognizes that traveling can be an opportunity to connect with local communities and learn about their customs and traditions. Therefore, it provides information on cultural experiences that promote cross-cultural understanding and respect.

Additionally, this guide acknowledges that Vienna is a city that is home to diverse communities, and visitors can benefit from learning about their perspectives and experiences. It provides information on events and activities that celebrate diversity and promote inclusivity.

Furthermore, this guide aims to provide visitors with information on local cuisine and dining options. Vienna is known for its rich culinary traditions, and visitors can sample a wide range of dishes from different regions and cultures. This guide provides recommendations on where to eat, as well as information on local customs and etiquette.

Lastly, this guide recognizes that traveling can be a transformative experience, and it aims to inspire visitors to explore beyond the city's main attractions and to engage with the city in a more meaningful way. It provides information on volunteering opportunities, as well as tips on how to support local businesses and initiatives.

In conclusion, the purpose of this guide is not only to help visitors plan a trip to Vienna in 2023 but also to encourage responsible and sustainable tourism practices. It aims to promote cross-cultural understanding, inclusivity, and respect for the natural environment. It provides information on local cuisine, volunteering opportunities, and sustainable travel practices. This guide aims to be a comprehensive resource that inspires visitors to have a meaningful and transformative experience in this beautiful city.

Background information on Vienna

Vienna is the capital and largest city of Austria, located in the heart of Europe. It is situated on the banks of the Danube River and is surrounded by the Vienna Woods, which offer stunning views of the city and its surroundings. Vienna is a city with a rich history, culture, and heritage, and it has played a significant role in shaping European history.

Vienna has been inhabited since the Roman era, and it has been a center of culture and commerce since the Middle Ages. In the 16th century, Vienna became the seat of the Habsburg dynasty, which ruled over the Austrian Empire and later the Austro-Hungarian Empire. During this period, Vienna became a hub of artistic and intellectual activity, and it attracted some of the most prominent artists, musicians, and thinkers of the time.

Vienna played a key role in European history during the 18th and 19th centuries. In 1815, Vienna hosted the Congress of Vienna, which aimed to re-establish peace and stability in Europe following the Napoleonic Wars. The city became the capital of the Austro-Hungarian Empire in 1867 and experienced a period of economic growth and cultural flourishing. During this time, Vienna became a center of modernism and attracted many artists and intellectuals who sought to challenge traditional artistic and cultural norms.

Vienna's rich cultural heritage can be seen in its stunning architecture, which reflects a range of styles from different historical periods. The city is home to numerous palaces, museums, and cultural institutions, including the Hofburg Palace, the Belvedere Palace, and the Kunsthistorisches Museum. Vienna is also known for its music, and it has been home to many famous composers, including Mozart, Beethoven, and Brahms. The city is home to the Vienna State Opera, which is renowned for its world-class performances.

Today, Vienna is a vibrant and dynamic city, known for its high quality of life, rich cultural heritage, and stunning natural scenery. It is a popular destination for tourists from around the world, and it offers a range of activities and attractions for visitors of all ages and interests. From its stunning architecture to its world-class museums and cultural institutions, Vienna is a city that is steeped in history, culture, and heritage, and it is a must-visit destination for anyone interested in exploring the best that Europe has to offer.

Vienna is also a city that values sustainability and environmental protection. It has been named the world's most livable city multiple times and has been recognized for its commitment to sustainability and eco-friendly practices. The city has an extensive public transportation system that includes buses, trams, and trains, making it easy for visitors to explore the city without relying on cars. Vienna also has numerous green spaces, including parks and gardens, that offer a respite from the hustle and bustle of the city.

In addition to its cultural and environmental attractions, Vienna is also known for its culinary traditions. The city's cuisine reflects its rich cultural heritage, and visitors can sample a wide range of dishes from different regions and cultures. Vienna is known for its coffee culture, and visitors can enjoy a cup of coffee at one of the city's many traditional coffeehouses. The city is also famous for its pastries, including the Sachertorte and Apfelstrudel.

Vienna is a city that offers something for everyone, whether you are interested in exploring its rich cultural heritage, enjoying its stunning natural scenery, or sampling its delicious cuisine. It is a city that is steeped in history, culture, and tradition, and it is a must-visit destination for anyone interested in experiencing the best that Europe has to offer. Whether you are a first-time visitor or a seasoned traveler, Vienna is a city that is sure to captivate and inspire you.

Vienna is also a city that is committed to innovation and creativity. It has a thriving startup scene and is home to many innovative companies and organizations. The city is known for its emphasis on research and development, and it has a number of world-class research institutions and universities. Vienna is also a city that values the arts and creativity, and it has a vibrant artistic community that includes painters, sculptors, writers, and musicians.

Another notable aspect of Vienna is its rich history of social and political movements. The city has played a key role in many important social and political movements throughout history, including the labor movement, women's rights movement, and environmental movement. Vienna is also known for its role in the fight against fascism and dictatorship, and it has been recognized for its commitment to democracy and human rights.

Overall, Vienna is a city with a rich and diverse history, culture, and heritage. It is a city that values sustainability, innovation, creativity, and social progress. It is a city that offers a unique blend of tradition and modernity, and it is a must-visit destination for anyone interested in experiencing the best that Europe has to offer.

When to visit Vienna

Vienna is a city that can be visited year-round, but the best time to visit depends on your preferences and interests. The city experiences four distinct seasons, with warm summers and cold winters.

Summer (June to August) is the peak tourist season in Vienna, and it is the time when the city is most crowded. The weather is warm and sunny, and there are many outdoor events and festivals, including the Vienna Jazz Festival and the Danube Island Festival. However, be prepared for high hotel prices and long lines at popular attractions.

Fall (September to November) is a great time to visit Vienna, as the weather is still mild, and the city is less crowded than in the summer. The fall foliage in the Vienna Woods is also a sight to behold, and there are many wine festivals and cultural events, including the Vienna Design Week and the Viennale Film Festival.

Winter (December to February) is a magical time to visit Vienna, with its Christmas markets and festive decorations. The city is also home to many world-class classical concerts during the holiday season, including the Vienna Philharmonic Orchestra's New Year's Day Concert. However, be prepared for cold temperatures and potentially snowy weather.

Spring (March to May) is another great time to visit Vienna, as the weather begins to warm up, and the city is less crowded than in the summer. The city is also known for its beautiful spring blooms, and there are many cultural events and festivals, including the Vienna City Marathon and the Vienna Festival.

Ultimately, the best time to visit Vienna depends on your interests and preferences. If you prefer warmer weather and outdoor events, then summer might be the best time to visit. However, if you prefer cooler temperatures and festive holiday events, then winter might be the perfect time for you. Regardless of when you visit, Vienna is a city that offers a unique and unforgettable experience.

In addition to the seasonal factors, it's worth considering Vienna's high and low tourism periods when planning your trip. July and August are the busiest months in Vienna when it comes to tourism, with peak hotel rates and crowds at popular attractions. The period from September to November and from March to May is a shoulder season in Vienna, where you can experience fewer crowds and lower hotel rates.

If you're looking for the best deals on hotels and flights, consider visiting Vienna during the low season, which is from December to February, except for the Christmas and New Year's period. During this time, you can enjoy lower hotel rates and fewer crowds at popular tourist sites. It's worth noting, however, that some attractions, such as outdoor markets and gardens, may have limited hours or may be closed during this time.

It's also important to keep in mind that Vienna is a popular destination for congresses and conferences, so it's worth checking the city's event calendar before booking your trip. Some of the largest events in Vienna include the Vienna International Film Festival in October, the Vienna Opera Ball in February, and the Vienna City Marathon in April.

No matter when you visit Vienna, you'll find a city that is rich in culture, history, and tradition. Whether you're exploring the city's stunning architecture, visiting its world-renowned museums and galleries, or sampling its delicious cuisine, Vienna is a city that offers a unique and unforgettable experience.

Chapter 2

Planning Your Trip

Planning a trip to Vienna can be an exciting and rewarding experience. Here are some tips to help you make the most of your visit to this beautiful city.

Determine the length of your stay: Vienna is a city that can be explored in a few days, but if you want to delve deeper into the culture and history of the city, plan for a longer stay. A week or more will give you ample time to see the top attractions, explore lesser-known neighborhoods, and enjoy the city's vibrant cultural scene.

Choose the right accommodation: Vienna has a range of accommodation options, from luxurious five-star hotels to cozy bed and breakfasts. Choose accommodation that suits your budget and preferences. Consider staying in the city center, which will give you easy access to the top attractions and public transportation.

Plan your itinerary: Vienna has an abundance of things to see and do, so plan your itinerary based on your interests and preferences. Don't miss the city's top attractions, such as the Schönbrunn Palace, St. Stephen's Cathedral, and the Vienna State Opera. Also, take some time to explore the lesser-known neighborhoods, such as Neubau and Leopoldstadt, to experience the local culture and cuisine.

Purchase a Vienna City Card: The Vienna City Card is a must-have for visitors to the city. It provides free transportation on public transit, discounts on top attractions, and special deals at restaurants and shops. It's an excellent way to save money while exploring the city.

Learn about the culture: Vienna has a rich cultural heritage, and learning about its history, traditions, and customs will enhance your visit. Attend a classical concert or opera performance, visit one of the city's many museums or galleries, or take a culinary tour to experience the local cuisine.

Consider a guided tour: A guided tour can be an excellent way to learn about the history and culture of Vienna. There are many tour companies offering walking tours, food tours, and cultural tours of the city. Choose a tour that suits your interests and preferences.

Check the weather: Vienna experiences four distinct seasons, so check the weather before you go. Pack appropriate clothing and footwear for the season and be prepared for sudden changes in weather.

By following these tips, you'll be able to plan a memorable and enjoyable trip to Vienna. With its rich culture, history, and cuisine, Vienna is a city that offers something for everyone.

Visa requirements

If you are planning a trip to Vienna, it is important to determine whether you need a visa to enter Austria. Visa requirements depend on your country of citizenship, the duration of your stay, and the purpose of your visit.

If you are a citizen of the European Union (EU) or European Economic Area (EEA), you do not need a visa to enter Austria. You can enter the country using your valid passport or national identity card. However, if you are a citizen of a non-EU country, you may need a visa depending on the length and purpose of your stay.

For short-term stays of up to 90 days within a 180-day period, citizens of some countries, including the United States, Canada, Australia, and Japan, do not need a visa to enter Austria. They can enter Austria as tourists, for business purposes, or for other short-term visits without a visa. However, if you are planning to work or study in Austria, you will need to apply for a visa.

To determine whether you need a visa for your visit to Austria, you should check the visa requirements for your country of citizenship. You can find this information on the website of the Austrian embassy or consulate in your home country. You can also contact the embassy or consulate directly to obtain more information and to apply for a visa if necessary.

When applying for a visa, you will need to provide documentation such as your passport, proof of travel arrangements, proof of accommodation, and proof of financial means to support your stay. You may also need to provide a letter of invitation from a sponsor or a letter from your employer or school.

It is important to apply for your visa well in advance of your travel dates, as the application process can take several weeks or even months. It is also important to ensure that you have all the necessary documentation and that you meet the requirements for the type of visa you are applying for.

In summary, if you are planning a visit to Vienna, it is important to determine whether you need a visa to enter Austria. Check the visa requirements for your country of citizenship and apply for a visa well in advance of your travel dates if necessary. With the proper documentation, you can enjoy a hassle-free trip to Vienna and experience all that this beautiful city has to offer.

In addition to checking visa requirements, it is important to also consider other factors when planning your trip to Vienna. For example, it is important to ensure that your passport is valid for at least six months beyond your intended departure date from Austria. If your passport is set to expire soon, you should renew it before your trip.

You should also consider purchasing travel insurance to protect yourself in case of unexpected events such as illness, injury, or trip cancellation. Travel insurance can provide coverage for medical expenses, emergency evacuation, and other travel-related expenses.

When booking your travel arrangements, it is important to consider the time of year you plan to visit Vienna. The peak tourist season in Vienna is from June to August, when the weather is warm and many outdoor events and festivals take place. However, this is also the busiest and most expensive time to visit. If you prefer to avoid crowds and save money, you may want to consider visiting during the shoulder seasons of April to May or September to October.

It is also important to consider the local customs and etiquette when visiting Vienna. Austrians place a high value on punctuality, so it is important to arrive on time for appointments and meetings. It is also customary to greet people with a handshake and to address them by their formal title and last name until invited to use their first name.

In summary, planning your trip to Vienna involves more than just checking visa requirements. It is important to consider factors such as passport validity, travel insurance, time of year, and local customs and etiquette. With proper planning and preparation, you can enjoy a smooth and enjoyable trip to Vienna.

Currency and exchange rate

The currency used in Vienna and Austria is the Euro (EUR). As a member of the European Union, Austria adopted the Euro in 2002, replacing the Austrian Schilling.

If you are traveling to Vienna from a country that does not use the Euro, you will need to exchange your currency for Euros. The exchange rate between your currency and the Euro can fluctuate depending on market conditions and economic factors. It is important to check the current exchange rate before you travel to Vienna to ensure that you have an accurate understanding of the value of your money.

There are several ways to exchange currency in Vienna. One option is to exchange currency at a bank or exchange office. Banks typically offer the most competitive exchange rates, but they may charge a commission or transaction fee for exchanging currency. Exchange offices, on the other hand, may offer a more convenient location but may charge higher fees or offer less favorable exchange rates.

Another option for exchanging currency is to use an ATM. ATMs are widely available throughout Vienna, and many accept foreign debit and credit cards. However, you should check with your bank or credit card company to see if they charge foreign transaction fees or ATM fees. It is also important to ensure that your debit or credit card has a chip and a PIN, as many European ATMs do not accept magnetic stripe cards or require a PIN for authentication.

When exchanging currency, it is important to be aware of scams and fraud. Avoid exchanging currency with street vendors or unlicensed exchange offices, as they may offer fraudulent or counterfeit currency. It is also important to count your currency carefully and to check for any discrepancies or errors before leaving the exchange office.

In summary, the Euro is the currency used in Vienna and Austria, and exchange rates can fluctuate depending on market conditions. There are several options for exchanging currency, including banks, exchange offices, and ATMs. When exchanging currency, it is important to be aware of fees, scams, and fraud, and to check the accuracy of your currency before leaving the exchange office.

It is also worth noting that many businesses in Vienna, especially larger ones such as hotels and tourist attractions, will accept credit cards as a form of payment. Visa and Mastercard are widely accepted, while American Express and Discover may not be accepted as widely.

When using a credit card in Vienna, it is important to inform your bank or credit card company of your travel plans in advance. This can help prevent your card from being flagged for fraud or unauthorized use. You should also check with your bank or credit card company to see if they charge foreign transaction fees, as these fees can add up quickly.

If you plan to use cash for smaller purchases or for transactions at local markets or street vendors, it is recommended to carry smaller denominations of Euro bills. This can make transactions easier and can help prevent overpaying for smaller items.

Finally, it is important to keep in mind that currency exchange rates can fluctuate frequently, so it is a good idea to monitor the exchange rate before and during your trip. This can help you make informed decisions about exchanging currency and can help you budget for your trip more effectively.

Transportation options

Vienna has a well-developed and efficient public transportation system that includes buses, trams, subways, and trains. The transportation system in Vienna is operated by Wiener Linien, which is responsible for managing and maintaining the network.

One of the most convenient and affordable ways to travel in Vienna is by using the subway, also known as the U-Bahn. The U-Bahn has five lines that connect different parts of the city and runs from approximately 5:00 a.m. until midnight. The trains are modern, clean, and air-conditioned, and provide quick and easy access to many of Vienna's top attractions.

Another option for public transportation in Vienna is the tram system. The tram network is extensive and covers most parts of the city, including the historic city center. The trams are a great way to see the city and provide a unique perspective on Vienna's streets and architecture.

Buses are also available in Vienna, but are typically slower and less frequent than the U-Bahn and tram systems. However, buses are a good option for reaching destinations that are not serviced by the subway or tram networks.

In addition to public transportation, taxis are also widely available in Vienna. Taxis are a convenient way to get around the city, especially if you are traveling in a group or have luggage. However, taxi fares in Vienna can be relatively expensive compared to public transportation options.

For longer distances or travel outside of Vienna, trains are a good option. Vienna has several train stations that connect the city to other parts of Austria and Europe. The main train station in Vienna is Wien Hauptbahnhof, which is the central hub for train travel in the city.

It is worth noting that Vienna is a very bike-friendly city, with many dedicated bike lanes and paths throughout the city. Biking is a great way to see the city and get some exercise at the same time. There are several bike rental companies in Vienna, making it easy to rent a bike and explore the city on your own.

In summary, Vienna has a well-developed and efficient public transportation system that includes subways, trams, buses, and trains. Taxis are also widely available, but can be relatively expensive. For longer distances or travel outside of Vienna, trains are a good option. Biking is also a popular option, with many dedicated bike lanes and paths throughout the city.

When using public transportation in Vienna, it is important to purchase a ticket or pass before boarding. Tickets can be purchased from ticket machines located at subway stations, tram stops, and bus stops. Single trip tickets and day passes are available, as well as weekly and monthly passes for frequent travelers.

Vienna also offers a convenient mobile app called WienMobil, which allows users to purchase tickets and passes directly from their mobile devices. The app also provides real-time information on public transportation schedules and routes.

Another transportation option in Vienna is the City Airport Train, or CAT. The CAT provides a direct connection from Vienna International Airport to the city center, with trains departing every 30 minutes. The CAT is a convenient and fast way to travel between the airport and the city, with a journey time of just 16 minutes.

For those who prefer to drive, it is important to keep in mind that parking in Vienna can be challenging and expensive. Many of the streets in the city center are pedestrianized or restricted to local traffic only. There are several public parking garages located throughout the city, but they can be expensive.

Overall, Vienna's public transportation system is a convenient and affordable way to get around the city, with options ranging from subways and trams to buses and trains. Taxis and the CAT provide additional options for transportation, while biking is a great way to see the city and get some exercise. When planning your trip to Vienna, it is important to consider your transportation options and choose the option that best fits your needs and budget.

One thing to keep in mind when using public transportation in Vienna is that smoking is strictly prohibited in all vehicles and stations. Additionally, it is important to validate your ticket before boarding the subway or tram. Ticket inspectors often patrol the vehicles and stations, and failure to have a valid ticket can result in a fine.

When taking a taxi in Vienna, it is important to check the fare before getting in the vehicle. Taxis in Vienna are required to have a meter, and the fare is based on the distance traveled and time of day. However, some unscrupulous taxi drivers may try to overcharge tourists, so it is important to be aware of the fare and any additional charges before starting your journey.

For those traveling outside of Vienna, it is worth considering the Eurail pass, which provides unlimited train travel in up to 33 European countries, including Austria. The pass can be a cost-effective option for those planning to travel extensively throughout Europe.

Overall, Vienna's transportation options provide travelers with a convenient and efficient way to get around the city and beyond. Whether you choose to use public transportation, taxis, or rent a bike, there are plenty of options to suit your needs and budget. By planning ahead and choosing the right transportation option, you can make the most of your time in Vienna and explore all that this beautiful city has to offer.

Accommodation options

Vienna offers a wide range of accommodation options to suit all budgets and preferences, from luxury hotels to budget hostels and everything in between. When planning your trip to Vienna, it is important to consider your accommodation options and choose the one that best fits your needs and budget.

Luxury hotels in Vienna offer world-class amenities and services, including spas, fitness centers, and gourmet restaurants. Some of the most well-known luxury hotels in Vienna include the Hotel Sacher, the Ritz-Carlton Vienna, and the Hotel Imperial.

For those on a budget, hostels and budget hotels provide affordable accommodation options in convenient locations throughout the city. Hostels offer shared dormitory-style rooms as well as private rooms with shared or private bathrooms. Some of the most popular hostels in Vienna include Wombat's City Hostels and MEININGER Hotel Vienna Downtown Franz.

Airbnb is also a popular accommodation option in Vienna, with a wide range of apartments and houses available for rent throughout the city. Airbnb allows travelers to stay in a home-like environment and experience local life in Vienna.

In addition to traditional hotels and hostels, Vienna also offers unique accommodation options such as boutique hotels, guesthouses, and apartments. These types of accommodations often provide a more personalized experience and are a great option for those who want to immerse themselves in local culture.

When choosing your accommodation in Vienna, it is important to consider factors such as location, amenities, and price. Vienna's public transportation system makes it easy to get around the city, so it is not necessary to stay in the city center. However, staying in the city center can provide easy access to Vienna's top attractions and nightlife.

Overall, Vienna offers a wide range of accommodation options to suit all budgets and preferences. By choosing the right accommodation for your needs and budget, you can ensure a comfortable and enjoyable stay in this beautiful city.

Vienna is a popular tourist destination, especially during peak seasons such as the summer months and the winter holiday season. Therefore, it is recommended to book your accommodation in advance to secure the best deals and availability.

Luxury hotels in Vienna often offer packages and deals during off-peak seasons, such as the spring and fall months. This can be a great option for those looking to experience the luxurious amenities of these hotels at a lower cost. On the other hand, budget accommodations tend to be more affordable year-round.

When choosing your accommodation in Vienna, it is also important to consider the type of experience you want to have. For example, staying in a historic hotel in Vienna's city center can provide a glimpse into the city's rich history and culture. Alternatively, staying in a trendy neighborhood such as the Mariahilf district can provide a more modern and vibrant experience.

Additionally, it is important to consider the amenities and services offered by your chosen accommodation. Some hotels offer 24-hour reception, airport transfers, and breakfast included in the price. Others may offer on-site restaurants and bars, fitness centers, and spa facilities.

Overall, Vienna offers a diverse range of accommodation options to suit all budgets and preferences. By doing your research and choosing the accommodation that best fits your needs and budget, you can ensure a comfortable and enjoyable stay in this beautiful city.

Types of accommodations

Vienna offers a diverse range of accommodation options to suit all budgets and preferences, from luxury hotels to budget hostels and everything in between. Here are some of the most popular types of accommodations in Vienna:

Luxury Hotels - Vienna is home to some of the world's most luxurious hotels, offering world-class amenities and services such as spas, fitness centers, and gourmet restaurants. Some of the most well-known luxury hotels in Vienna include the Hotel Sacher, the Ritz-Carlton Vienna, and the Hotel Imperial.

Boutique Hotels - Boutique hotels in Vienna offer a unique and personalized experience, often located in historic buildings with stylish decor and unique features. These hotels may offer amenities such as on-site restaurants and bars, and often provide a more intimate atmosphere than larger chain hotels.

Budget Hotels - Budget hotels in Vienna provide affordable accommodation options in convenient locations throughout the city. They may offer basic amenities such as free Wi-Fi and breakfast, and some may have shared bathrooms.

Hostels - Hostels in Vienna offer a variety of room types, from shared dormitory-style rooms to private rooms with shared or private bathrooms. They provide affordable accommodation options for budget-conscious travelers, and often have communal areas where guests can socialize.

Guesthouses - Guesthouses in Vienna offer a more home-like atmosphere than hotels, often located in residential neighborhoods. They provide basic amenities such as free Wi-Fi and breakfast, and some may have communal areas for guests to socialize.

Apartments - Apartments in Vienna provide a more independent experience, with fully equipped kitchens and the ability to cook your own meals. They are a great option for families or groups traveling together, and often offer more space than traditional hotel rooms.

Airbnb - Airbnb is a popular accommodation option in Vienna, with a wide range of apartments and houses available for rent throughout the city. Airbnb allows travelers to stay in a home-like environment and experience local life in Vienna.

When choosing your accommodation in Vienna, it is important to consider factors such as location, amenities, and price. Each type of accommodation has its own advantages and disadvantages, and it is important to choose the option that best fits your needs and budget.

Luxury Hotels

Vienna is known for its luxurious hotels that offer world-class amenities and services. These hotels are often located in historic buildings with elegant architecture, providing guests with a glimpse into the city's rich history and culture. Here are some of the best luxury hotels in Vienna:

Hotel Sacher - The Hotel Sacher is one of the most famous luxury hotels in Vienna, located in the heart of the city near the State Opera House. The hotel has been family-owned for over 150 years and is known for its luxurious rooms and suites, elegant decor, and gourmet dining options.

Ritz-Carlton Vienna - The Ritz-Carlton Vienna is a five-star hotel located in a historic building on the famous Ringstrasse Boulevard. The hotel features 202 luxurious rooms and suites, a rooftop bar with stunning views of the city, and a wellness center with a sauna, steam room, and fitness center.

Hotel Imperial - The Hotel Imperial is a historic luxury hotel located in the heart of Vienna's city center. The hotel features 138 luxurious rooms and suites, many of which are decorated with antique furniture and artwork. The hotel also has a gourmet restaurant, a bar, and a spa.

Park Hyatt Vienna - The Park Hyatt Vienna is a five-star hotel located in a historic building near St. Stephen's Cathedral. The hotel features 143 luxurious rooms and suites, a spa with an indoor pool, a gourmet restaurant, and a bar.

Palais Hansen Kempinski Vienna - The Palais Hansen Kempinski Vienna is a luxury hotel located in a historic building near the Danube Canal. The hotel features 152 luxurious rooms and suites, a gourmet restaurant, a bar, and a spa with an indoor pool and sauna.

These luxury hotels in Vienna offer a range of amenities and services, including 24-hour room service, concierge services, and fitness centers. They are known for their elegant decor, attention to detail, and personalized service, making them a top choice for discerning travelers seeking a luxurious experience in Vienna.

Hotel Sacher -

The Hotel Sacher is one of the most iconic luxury hotels in Vienna and has a rich history that spans over 150 years. The hotel was founded in 1876 by Eduard Sacher, the son of the famous pastry chef who created the famous Sachertorte cake.

The original Hotel Sacher was located in a different building than the current one and was known for its luxurious amenities and grand decor. The hotel quickly became a popular destination for high society and the wealthy elite, with guests including politicians, artists, and musicians.

In 1880, the Hotel Sacher was acquired by the Gürtler and Winkler families, who expanded the hotel and added modern amenities such as electricity, central heating, and elevators. The hotel was also home to a famous restaurant that served traditional Viennese cuisine, as well as the famous Sachertorte cake.

During World War II, the Hotel Sacher was severely damaged and was forced to close its doors for several years. In 1947, the hotel was rebuilt and reopened with a new location near the State Opera House.

Over the years, the Hotel Sacher has hosted many notable guests, including Queen Elizabeth II, John F. Kennedy, and Indira Gandhi. The hotel has also been featured in several films, including "The Third Man" and "Mission: Impossible - Rogue Nation".

Today, the Hotel Sacher remains one of the most prestigious luxury hotels in Vienna, known for its elegant decor, world-class amenities, and exceptional service. The hotel features 149 luxurious rooms and suites, several restaurants and bars, a spa and fitness center, and a range of amenities to cater to the needs of discerning travelers. The hotel is still owned and operated by the Gürtler and Winkler families, ensuring that the hotel's legacy and commitment to excellence continue to thrive.

The hotel is located on the famous Kärntner Straße, within walking distance of Vienna's best attractions, including the Vienna State Opera, St. Stephen's Cathedral, and the Hofburg Palace. The hotel is also conveniently located near public transportation, making it easy to explore the city.

One of the main reasons to stay at Hotel Sacher is the hotel's rich history and tradition. The hotel is known for its excellent service and timeless elegance. From the moment you arrive, you will be greeted with the warmth and friendliness that is a hallmark of Austrian hospitality. The hotel's opulent interior is decorated with exquisite art pieces and antiques, giving you a glimpse of Vienna's rich cultural heritage.

The hotel has 149 rooms and suites, each individually decorated in a classic Viennese style. The rooms are spacious, comfortable, and feature luxurious amenities, including a marble bathroom, a flat-screen TV, and complimentary Wi-Fi. The hotel's suites are particularly impressive, featuring separate living areas, fireplaces, and stunning views of the city.

In addition to the hotel's luxurious rooms, Hotel Sacher offers exceptional dining experiences. The hotel is home to two restaurants, both of which have been awarded Michelin stars. The first is the famous Café Sacher Wien, which is renowned for its original Sacher Torte cake. This Viennese delicacy is a must-try when visiting the city, and the café is the perfect place to enjoy it. The second restaurant is the Anna Sacher, which serves classic Viennese cuisine in an elegant setting.

Hotel Sacher also boasts an impressive wellness center, which includes a sauna, steam room, and a fitness center. The hotel's spa offers a range of treatments, including massages and beauty treatments. Guests can relax in the hotel's library or enjoy a drink at the hotel's bar.

Finally, the hotel's location is perfect for exploring Vienna. The hotel is located in the heart of the city, making it easy to explore Vienna's best attractions, including the Vienna State Opera, St. Stephen's Cathedral, and the Hofburg Palace. The hotel is also located near public transportation, making it easy to explore the city's other neighborhoods and attractions.

In conclusion, Hotel Sacher is an excellent choice for travelers looking for a luxurious and authentic Viennese experience. The hotel's rich history, elegant decor, exceptional dining experiences, and impressive wellness center make it an ideal choice for those looking to immerse themselves in Vienna's cultural heritage. Whether you are traveling for business or pleasure, Hotel Sacher is sure to exceed your expectations and provide you with a memorable stay in one of Europe's most beautiful cities.

Ritz-Carlton Vienna -

The Ritz-Carlton Vienna is a luxurious hotel located in the heart of the city, with a rich history that dates back to the early 20th century.

Originally built in 1913 as the Hotel Imperial, the building was designed by architect Arnold Heymann, who also designed several other iconic buildings in Vienna. The Hotel Imperial quickly became known for its opulence and grandeur, with guests including royalty, politicians, and celebrities.

During World War II, the hotel was used as a military hospital by the German army. After the war, the hotel was seized by the Soviet Union, and it was not until 1955 that the hotel was returned to its original owners.

In the years following World War II, the hotel underwent several renovations and changes of ownership. In the 1970s, the hotel was purchased by a group of investors and renamed the InterContinental Vienna.

In 2012, the building underwent a major renovation and was transformed into the Ritz-Carlton Vienna. The hotel now features 202 guest rooms and suites, as well as a variety of amenities, including a fitness center, spa, and several dining options.

Despite the changes and renovations over the years, the Ritz-Carlton Vienna has managed to maintain its original grandeur and charm. Many of the hotel's original features and furnishings have been preserved, including the ornate marble staircase and the historic ballroom, which is now used for events and weddings.

Today, the Ritz-Carlton Vienna is one of the most luxurious hotels in the city, attracting high-end travelers from around the world. The hotel's rich history and classic elegance make it a popular destination for those looking for a true Viennese experience.

The Ritz-Carlton Vienna has become synonymous with luxury and sophistication, offering guests a unique blend of history, modern amenities, and personalized service. The hotel's prime location in the heart of the city makes it an ideal base for exploring Vienna's many cultural and historical attractions, including the nearby State Opera House, St. Stephen's Cathedral, and Hofburg Palace.

The Ritz-Carlton Vienna features 202 elegantly designed guest rooms and suites, each with its own unique charm and style. Rooms are equipped with luxurious amenities, including flat-screen TVs, marble bathrooms, plush bedding, and complimentary Wi-Fi.

In addition to its luxurious accommodations, the Ritz-Carlton Vienna offers a range of dining options to suit all tastes and occasions. The hotel's signature restaurant, Dstrikt Steakhouse, serves up a range of premium cuts of meat, along with local and international dishes, in a chic and sophisticated setting. The hotel's lobby lounge and bar, Melounge, is the perfect spot for a relaxing drink or afternoon tea.

The Ritz-Carlton Vienna also features a state-of-the-art fitness center and spa, which offers a range of indulgent treatments and therapies, including massages, facials, and body treatments. Guests can also enjoy the hotel's indoor pool and sauna facilities.

With its rich history and classic elegance, the Ritz-Carlton Vienna is the perfect destination for those looking for a luxurious and unforgettable stay in one of Europe's most beautiful and culturally rich cities. Whether you're traveling for business or leisure, the hotel's world-class amenities, personalized service, and prime location make it the perfect choice for discerning travelers.

Hotel Imperial -

The Hotel Imperial is one of the most iconic and historic hotels in Vienna. The hotel was originally built in 1863 as a palace for the Duke of Württemberg, but it was later sold to the Imperial and Royal Court in 1873, becoming the residence of Prince Philip of Württemberg. It was then transformed into a luxury hotel in 1876 to accommodate the increasing number of travelers to Vienna.

The hotel's location on the prestigious Ringstrasse, which is known for its stunning architecture and rich history, made it an ideal destination for royalty, aristocrats, and celebrities visiting the city. Many of the hotel's guests were members of the royal families of Europe, including Queen Elizabeth of England, the Emperor of Japan, and the Shah of Persia.

During World War II, the Hotel Imperial was requisitioned by the Nazi regime and used as a military headquarters. After the war, the hotel was restored and reopened as a luxury hotel, and it once again became a popular destination for high-profile guests.

Over the years, the Hotel Imperial has undergone several renovations and expansions to maintain its luxurious standards and preserve its historic character. In 2000, the hotel underwent a major renovation, which added modern amenities and updated the hotel's infrastructure while maintaining its original architectural style.

Today, the Hotel Imperial continues to be one of the most prestigious and luxurious hotels in Vienna. The hotel's lavish guest rooms and suites are decorated in a classic Viennese style, with ornate details, antique furnishings, and modern amenities. The hotel's Imperial restaurant is also renowned for its traditional Austrian cuisine, while the Cafe Imperial serves some of the best coffee and pastries in the city.

Overall, the Hotel Imperial's rich history, stunning architecture, and luxurious amenities make it a top choice for travelers looking for an unforgettable and authentic Viennese experience.

Park Hyatt Vienna -

The Park Hyatt Vienna is a luxury hotel located in the heart of Vienna, Austria. The hotel is housed in a beautifully restored 100-year-old building that was once the headquarters of the Bank of Austria. The building itself is a work of art, with stunning Renaissance-style architecture and beautiful detailing.

The hotel opened its doors in 2014, after an extensive restoration that took more than three years to complete. The renovation was carried out by a team of architects, designers, and craftsmen who worked tirelessly to preserve the historic features of the building while incorporating modern amenities and luxurious touches.

The Park Hyatt Vienna is home to 143 rooms and suites, each of which is exquisitely decorated with elegant furnishings and luxurious amenities. The rooms feature high ceilings, large windows, and beautiful views of the city, creating a spacious and comfortable environment for guests to relax and unwind.

In addition to its luxurious accommodations, the Park Hyatt Vienna is also known for its exceptional dining experiences. The hotel's restaurant, The Bank Brasserie & Bar, offers a menu of classic Viennese dishes and international cuisine created by Executive Chef Stefan Resch. The restaurant's elegant decor and ambiance provide the perfect setting for a romantic dinner or a celebratory meal.

The hotel also has a beautiful bar, named The Living Room, where guests can enjoy a selection of cocktails, fine wines, and delicious snacks. The bar's stunning decor, which features a fireplace, comfortable seating, and an elegant atmosphere, creates a warm and inviting environment for guests to relax and socialize.

One of the highlights of the Park Hyatt Vienna is its spa and wellness center, which offers a range of treatments and services designed to promote relaxation and rejuvenation. The spa features a pool, sauna, steam room, and fitness center, as well as a variety of massage and beauty treatments.

Overall, the Park Hyatt Vienna is a stunning example of Viennese luxury and hospitality. Its rich history, beautiful architecture, exceptional service, and world-class amenities make it a must-visit destination for anyone traveling to Vienna. Whether you're looking for a romantic getaway, a relaxing spa vacation, or a luxurious business trip, the Park Hyatt Vienna has something to offer for everyone.

Palais Hansen Kempinski Vienna -

The Palais Hansen Kempinski Vienna is a luxurious hotel located in the heart of the city, just a short walk from some of Vienna's most famous landmarks. The hotel is housed in a historic building that was originally built in the late 19th century as a hotel for the World Exhibition held in Vienna in 1873.

The building was designed by Theophil von Hansen, a prominent Austrian architect who was responsible for designing many of Vienna's most iconic buildings. The hotel was named after Hansen, and it quickly became one of the city's most popular places to stay.

Over the years, the hotel went through a number of changes and renovations, with several different owners and operators taking over the property. During World War II, the building was badly damaged, and it took several years of restoration work to bring it back to its former glory.

In 2013, the building was taken over by the Kempinski group, a renowned luxury hotel brand that operates some of the world's most prestigious hotels. The Kempinski group embarked on a massive renovation project to transform the building into a world-class hotel, while still preserving its historic charm and character.

Today, the Palais Hansen Kempinski Vienna is a stunning hotel that combines historic elegance with modern luxury. The hotel features 152 luxurious rooms and suites, each of which is uniquely designed with a blend of classic and contemporary styles.

The public spaces of the hotel are equally impressive, with grand halls, sweeping staircases, and beautiful chandeliers adorning the interior. The hotel also features a range of dining options, including the Michelin-starred restaurant Edvard, which serves modern Austrian cuisine, and the Lobby Lounge, which offers a selection of afternoon teas and light snacks.

In addition to its luxurious accommodations and amenities, the Palais Hansen Kempinski Vienna is also renowned for its commitment to sustainability and environmental responsibility. The hotel has implemented a range of initiatives to reduce its environmental impact, including using energy-efficient lighting, sourcing locally produced food and beverages, and minimizing water consumption.

Overall, the Palais Hansen Kempinski Vienna is a truly exceptional hotel that offers guests a luxurious and unforgettable stay in one of Europe's most beautiful and historic cities. Its rich history, stunning architecture, and exceptional service make it a truly special place to stay while visiting Vienna.

Boutique Hotels -

Boutique hotels are a type of accommodation that have gained popularity in recent years, particularly among travelers seeking unique and personalized experiences. These hotels are characterized by their small size, stylish design, and attention to detail. Boutique hotels often have fewer than 100 rooms and are typically independently owned and operated, allowing for a more personalized experience for guests.

Boutique hotels often offer a high level of luxury and comfort, with attention paid to every aspect of the guest experience. From the design of the rooms and public spaces to the quality of the amenities and the level of service provided, every detail is carefully considered to create a unique and memorable experience for guests.

One of the defining features of boutique hotels is their unique design and aesthetic. These hotels often have a distinctive style, with each room or suite individually decorated to create a unique and welcoming atmosphere. Many boutique hotels incorporate elements of local culture and history into their design, giving guests a sense of place and a deeper connection to the destination.

In addition to their stylish design and personalized service, boutique hotels often offer a range of amenities and services designed to enhance the guest experience. These may include on-site restaurants or bars, fitness centers or spas, and unique experiences like cooking classes or local tours.

Boutique hotels can be found in cities and destinations around the world, from trendy neighborhoods in major cities to remote locations in the countryside or by the beach. They offer a unique and memorable way to experience a destination, with a focus on luxury, comfort, and individualized attention.

If you're looking for a unique and memorable travel experience, a boutique hotel may be the perfect choice. With their stylish design, personalized service, and attention to detail, these hotels offer a one-of-a-kind experience that will stay with you long after you leave.

Budget Hotels -

Vienna offers a wide range of budget-friendly accommodations for visitors who want to explore the city without breaking the bank. Budget hotels are a great option for those who are looking for a comfortable place to stay at an affordable price.

Most budget hotels in Vienna are located in the city center, close to major tourist attractions, restaurants, and shops. They offer basic amenities such as free Wi-Fi, TV, and a private bathroom. Some budget hotels also provide breakfast for an additional fee.

One of the most popular budget hotels in Vienna is the Wombat's City Hostel. With locations in the Naschmarkt and the Westbahnhof, this hostel offers dormitory rooms with shared bathrooms and private rooms with en-suite bathrooms. The hostel also provides a free breakfast buffet, a rooftop bar, and a communal kitchen for guests to use.

Another budget-friendly option is the A&O Wien Hauptbahnhof. This hostel is located close to the main train station and offers both private and shared rooms with free Wi-Fi and a private bathroom. Guests can also enjoy the hostel's bar and lounge area, as well as its game room and outdoor terrace.

For travelers who prefer a more traditional hotel experience, the Ibis Wien Mariahilf is a great choice. This hotel is located in the trendy Mariahilfer Strasse shopping district and offers comfortable rooms with free Wi-Fi and a private bathroom. Guests can also enjoy the hotel's bar and restaurant, as well as its convenient location near public transportation.

Overall, budget hotels in Vienna provide a great option for travelers who want to save money on accommodations without sacrificing comfort and convenience. With a variety of options available throughout the city, visitors can find the perfect budget-friendly hotel for their needs.

When it comes to budget hotels in Vienna, travelers have many options to choose from. These hotels offer basic amenities and comfortable rooms at affordable prices, making them an ideal choice for budget-conscious travelers who are looking for a place to stay while exploring the city.

One popular budget hotel in Vienna is A&O Wien Hauptbahnhof. Located just a short walk from the city's main train station, this hotel offers both private rooms and dormitory-style accommodations. The hotel features a bar, a lounge, and a game room, as well as a 24-hour front desk and luggage storage.

Another budget-friendly option is the MEININGER Hotel Wien Downtown Sissi. This hotel is located in the heart of Vienna's second district and is just a short walk from the city center. The hotel offers a variety of room types, including dormitory-style accommodations, as well as a bar, a lounge, and a game room.

For those looking for a more traditional hotel experience, the Hotel Austria is a great option. This hotel is located in the city's fourth district and is just a short walk from the city center. The hotel features a restaurant, a bar, and a lounge, as well as a 24-hour front desk and luggage storage.

Other budget hotels in Vienna include the Ibis Wien Hauptbahnhof, the 25hours Hotel beim MuseumsQuartier, and the Motel One Wien-Staatsoper. No matter which budget hotel you choose, you can rest assured that you'll be able to enjoy all that Vienna has to offer without breaking the bank.

Hostels

Vienna is a great city to visit for travelers on a budget, and there are plenty of hostel options available. Hostels offer affordable accommodations with shared facilities, making them a great option for solo travelers or groups on a tight budget. Here are some of the best hostels in Vienna:

Wombats City Hostel Vienna: Wombats is a popular hostel chain in Europe, and their Vienna location is no exception. The hostel is located in a renovated 19th-century building and offers a variety of room options, including dorms and private rooms. Facilities include a bar, kitchen, laundry facilities, and a terrace with views of the city.

MEININGER Hotel Vienna Downtown Franz: MEININGER is a hybrid hotel-hostel that offers affordable accommodations with a range of room options, from dorms to private rooms with en-suite bathrooms. The hostel is located in the city center and has a shared kitchen, lounge, and game room.

Hostel Ruthensteiner Vienna: Hostel Ruthensteiner is a family-owned hostel that has been operating for over 50 years. The hostel offers a variety of room options, including dorms and private rooms with shared facilities. The hostel has a garden, common room, kitchen, and laundry facilities.

Hostel Hütteldorf: Hostel Hütteldorf is located on the outskirts of Vienna, but is easily accessible by public transportation. The hostel offers dorms and private rooms with shared facilities, as well as a kitchen, lounge, and outdoor terrace.

Do Step Inn: Do Step Inn is located in the trendy Neubau neighborhood and offers a variety of room options, including dorms and private rooms with shared facilities. The hostel has a common room, kitchen, and outdoor terrace.

Hostels in Vienna are generally clean, safe, and well-maintained, and offer a great value for travelers on a budget. Many hostels also offer social activities and events, making them a great option for solo travelers looking to meet other like-minded travelers.

Wombats City Hostel Vienna:

Wombats City Hostel Vienna is a popular hostel in the city that offers affordable accommodation for travelers on a budget. The hostel is located in the heart of Vienna and is just a short walk from some of the city's most popular tourist attractions, including St. Stephen's Cathedral and the Hofburg Palace.

The history of Wombats City Hostel Vienna dates back to 1999 when the first Wombats Hostel opened in Munich, Germany. The hostel was founded by three friends, Marcus, Sascha, and Stephan, who were all avid travelers themselves and wanted to create a hostel that offered a unique and enjoyable experience for their guests.

The success of the Munich hostel led to the opening of additional Wombats Hostels in Berlin, Budapest, and Vienna. Wombats City Hostel Vienna was opened in 2011 and has been providing travelers with a comfortable and affordable place to stay ever since.

The hostel is housed in a beautifully renovated building that dates back to the 19th century. The building was originally a hotel and was converted into a hostel in the early 2000s. The interior of the hostel is modern and stylish, with bright colors and unique design elements.

Wombats City Hostel Vienna offers a range of accommodation options, including dorm rooms and private rooms. All of the rooms are clean, comfortable, and equipped with modern amenities such as free Wi-Fi and lockers for secure storage.

One of the unique features of Wombats City Hostel Vienna is the large and inviting common area. This space is a great place for guests to relax, socialize, and meet other travelers from around the world. The common area includes a bar, a lounge area with comfortable seating, and a fully equipped kitchen for guests to use.

Overall, Wombats City Hostel Vienna is a great choice for travelers looking for affordable accommodation in the heart of the city. The hostel offers a unique and enjoyable experience, with a friendly and welcoming atmosphere that will make guests feel right at home.

MEININGER Hotel Vienna Downtown Franz:

MEININGER Hotel Vienna Downtown Franz is a modern hostel located in the heart of Vienna, just a few steps away from the city's main attractions. The hostel is named after the famous Emperor Franz Joseph I of Austria, who ruled from 1848 until his death in 1916.

The history of the building dates back to the early 20th century when it was used as a wine and spirits storage facility. In the 1950s, it was converted into a hotel and remained so until the MEININGER group took over the building and transformed it into a hostel in 2011.

MEININGER Hotel Vienna Downtown Franz is a popular choice for budget travelers who are looking for affordable and comfortable accommodation in the city center. The hostel offers a range of room options including dormitories, private rooms, and family rooms, all equipped with modern amenities such as free Wi-Fi, lockers, and ensuite bathrooms.

In addition to the comfortable accommodation, MEININGER Hotel Vienna Downtown Franz also offers a range of facilities and services for guests, including a 24-hour reception, a guest kitchen, a bar, and a lounge area. Guests can also enjoy a hearty breakfast buffet in the morning, and a range of snacks and drinks throughout the day.

The hostel's central location makes it the perfect base for exploring Vienna's many attractions, including St. Stephen's Cathedral, the Hofburg Palace, and the Vienna State Opera. Guests can also take a stroll along the famous shopping street Mariahilfer Straße or relax in the nearby Stadtpark.

MEININGER Hotel Vienna Downtown Franz has won several awards for its outstanding service and hospitality. The hostel's staff is known for their friendly and helpful attitude, ensuring that guests have a comfortable and enjoyable stay in the Austrian capital.

Hostel Ruthensteiner Vienna:

Hostel Ruthensteiner Vienna is one of the oldest and most famous hostels in the city. It was established in 1968 by an Austrian family who wanted to create a comfortable and affordable place for travelers to stay. Over the years, the hostel has undergone several renovations to keep up with the changing times and to meet the needs of modern travelers.

In the early days, Hostel Ruthensteiner was a small, family-run business that welcomed backpackers from around the world. It quickly gained a reputation as a friendly and welcoming place where travelers could meet other like-minded people and share their experiences. The hostel was originally located in a small building near Westbahnhof train station, but it quickly outgrew this space and had to be moved to a larger location in the city.

In the 1990s, the hostel underwent a major renovation that transformed it from a basic backpackers' hostel into a modern and stylish accommodation option. The building was completely refurbished, and new facilities were added to make the hostel more comfortable and convenient for guests. Today, Hostel Ruthensteiner is a popular choice for travelers who want to experience Vienna on a budget, but who still want to stay in comfortable and stylish surroundings.

One of the key features of Hostel Ruthensteiner is its unique and eclectic design. The hostel is decorated with a mix of modern and vintage furniture, and the walls are covered with colorful murals and artwork. The design of the hostel is inspired by the vibrant and creative spirit of Vienna, and it reflects the city's rich cultural heritage.

Despite its long history, Hostel Ruthensteiner has not lost its welcoming and friendly atmosphere. The staff are known for their warm and helpful attitude, and they go out of their way to ensure that guests have a comfortable and enjoyable stay. The hostel also offers a range of amenities, including free Wi-Fi, a fully equipped kitchen, and a cozy common room where guests can relax and socialize.

Overall, Hostel Ruthensteiner is a great choice for travelers who want to experience Vienna on a budget, without sacrificing comfort or style. Its long history and unique design make it a memorable and enjoyable place to stay, and its friendly staff are always on hand to offer advice and assistance.

Hostel Hütteldorf:

Hostel Hütteldorf is a popular hostel located in the Hütteldorf district of Vienna, Austria. The hostel is housed in a renovated, historic building that dates back to the 18th century. Originally built as a mansion, the building was later converted into a hospital before being transformed into a hostel in 1994.

The history of the building dates back to 1746, when it was built as a baroque-style mansion. The mansion was owned by a wealthy Viennese family, who used it as their summer residence. The mansion was known for its stunning gardens, which were designed in the French style.

In the early 19th century, the mansion was sold to the Austrian government, which converted it into a hospital. During this time, the building underwent significant renovations to accommodate patients. The hospital remained in operation until the early 1990s, when it was closed due to its outdated facilities.

In 1994, the building was purchased by a group of entrepreneurs who saw the potential for a hostel in the Hütteldorf district. The building was renovated and transformed into Hostel Hütteldorf, which quickly became a popular destination for backpackers and budget travelers.

Today, Hostel Hütteldorf offers a range of accommodations, including private rooms and dormitories. The hostel also features a common room, kitchen facilities, and a courtyard garden. Guests can enjoy easy access to Vienna's city center, as the hostel is located just a short walk from the Hütteldorf metro station.

The history and character of the building are evident throughout Hostel Hütteldorf. From the baroque architecture to the remnants of its hospital days, the hostel offers a unique and memorable experience for travelers. Its rich history and convenient location make Hostel Hütteldorf a popular choice for visitors to Vienna.

Do Step Inn:

Do Step Inn is a hostel located in the heart of Vienna, Austria. It was established in 2004 with the aim of providing affordable yet comfortable accommodation for travelers, backpackers, and students. The hostel is known for its welcoming atmosphere and convenient location, making it a popular choice for visitors to Vienna.

The history of Do Step Inn dates back to the early 2000s when the founders of the hostel identified a need for budget accommodation in Vienna. They wanted to create a space where travelers could enjoy a comfortable stay without breaking the bank. After months of planning and preparation, Do Step Inn opened its doors in 2004.

Since then, the hostel has undergone several renovations and upgrades to improve the comfort and facilities for guests. Today, Do Step Inn offers a range of rooms to suit different needs and budgets. From dormitory-style rooms with bunk beds to private rooms with en suite bathrooms, the hostel has something for everyone.

One of the unique features of Do Step Inn is its focus on sustainability and eco-friendliness. The hostel uses renewable energy sources such as solar panels and has implemented various measures to reduce its carbon footprint. For example, they encourage guests to conserve water and electricity and have installed energy-efficient appliances throughout the hostel.

Do Step Inn also prides itself on its community-oriented atmosphere. The hostel organizes regular events and activities for guests, including cultural tours, pub crawls, and social gatherings. This creates a welcoming environment where travelers can meet like-minded individuals and experience Vienna's vibrant culture.

In addition to its amenities and community spirit, Do Step Inn's location is a major draw for visitors to Vienna. The hostel is situated in the trendy Neubau district, known for its bohemian cafes, bars, and shops. It is also within walking distance of several major tourist attractions, including the Museumsquartier and the famous Naschmarkt.

Overall, the history of Do Step Inn is a testament to the power of a good idea and strong community spirit. By providing affordable, sustainable, and welcoming accommodation, the hostel has become a beloved institution in Vienna's travel scene.

Packing list

When it comes to travel, packing can be one of the most stressful parts of the journey. You want to make sure you have everything you need, but you also don't want to overpack and end up lugging around a heavy suitcase. Here's a well-detailed packing list to help ensure you have all the essentials for your trip.

Travel Documents:

Passport or ID

Visa (if required)

Printed copy of your travel itinerary

Printed copies of any hotel or tour reservations

Travel insurance documents

Money and Payment Options:

Credit or debit cards

Cash

Traveler's checks

Currency conversion app

Clothing:

Comfortable walking shoes

Lightweight jacket or coat

Sweater or cardigan

Comfortable pants or jeans

Shorts or skirts (if weather permits)

T-shirts or blouses

Socks and underwear

Pajamas

Swimwear (if you're going to a beach destination)

Dressy outfit for formal events (if required)

Toiletries:

Toothbrush and toothpaste

Hairbrush or comb

Shampoo and conditioner

Body wash or soap

Razor and shaving cream

Moisturizer

Sunscreen

Insect repellent

Medications and vitamins

First aid kit

Electronics:

Phone and charger

Camera and charger

Extra batteries or power bank

Travel adapter and voltage converter

Laptop or tablet (if necessary)

Miscellaneous:

Travel-sized laundry detergent (if planning to do laundry)

Umbrella or rain jacket

Travel pillow and eye mask

Lightweight daypack or tote bag

Water bottle

Snacks

Guidebook or travel apps

Maps and city guides

Travel locks for luggage

Portable luggage scale

It's always a good idea to pack light and avoid bringing unnecessary items. Keep in mind the weather and cultural customs of your destination when deciding what to pack. With this packing list, you can rest assured that you have everything you need for a comfortable and enjoyable trip.

Chapter 3

Top Tourist Attractions

Vienna, Austria is a beautiful city filled with history, culture, and architecture. Whether you're visiting for a short weekend or a longer stay, there are plenty of tourist attractions to explore. Here are some of the top tourist attractions in Vienna:

Schönbrunn Palace: This beautiful palace was the summer residence of the Habsburg monarchs and is now a UNESCO World Heritage Site. Visitors can tour the palace and its gardens, and even see the rooms where Mozart once performed.

Hofburg Palace: This sprawling palace complex was the imperial residence of the Habsburg dynasty for centuries. Today, visitors can explore the palace's museums and see the famous Spanish Riding School.

St. Stephen's Cathedral: This beautiful Gothic cathedral is one of Vienna's most iconic landmarks. Visitors can climb the tower for a stunning view of the city, or explore the cathedral's intricate architecture.

Belvedere Palace: This baroque palace was once the residence of Prince Eugene of Savoy and now houses a world-renowned art museum. Visitors can see works by Gustav Klimt and other famous artists.

Vienna State Opera: The Vienna State Opera is one of the world's most famous opera houses, with a rich history dating back to the 19th century. Visitors can take a tour of the opera house or see a live performance.

Naschmarkt: This lively market is a great place to experience Vienna's culinary scene. Visitors can try traditional Austrian dishes, as well as food from around the world.

Kunsthistorisches Museum: This impressive museum houses an extensive collection of art and artifacts from ancient Egypt, Greece, and Rome, as well as European paintings and sculptures.

Prater: This amusement park is a great place to have fun with the whole family. Visitors can ride the iconic Ferris wheel or try other thrilling rides.

Vienna Zoo: This zoo is the oldest in the world and is home to a wide variety of animals, including giant pandas, elephants, and tigers.

Danube River: The Danube River runs through Vienna and offers a beautiful setting for a leisurely walk or bike ride. Visitors can also take a boat tour and see the city from the water.

These are just a few of the many tourist attractions that Vienna has to offer. Whether you're interested in history, culture, art, or just having fun, there is something for everyone in this beautiful city.

Schönbrunn Palace

Schönbrunn Palace is one of the most popular tourist destinations in Vienna, Austria. Its history dates back to the late 17th century, when Emperor Leopold I commissioned the construction of a hunting lodge on the site. In 1696, the lodge was expanded and transformed into a palace, which served as the summer residence of the Habsburg emperors until 1918.

In the early 18th century, under the reign of Emperor Charles VI, Schönbrunn Palace underwent a significant renovation and expansion. The palace was redesigned in the Baroque style, with impressive facades, opulent interiors, and vast gardens. The most notable addition during this period was the Gloriette, a grandiose pavilion on a hill overlooking the palace.

During the reign of Empress Maria Theresa in the mid-18th century, Schönbrunn Palace became the center of court life and the stage for many important events, such as imperial weddings, diplomatic meetings, and concerts. The palace was also home to the Empress's large family, including her son, the future Emperor Joseph II.

In the 19th century, under the reign of Emperor Franz Joseph I, Schönbrunn Palace underwent another renovation, this time in the Neoclassical style. The palace's interiors were redesigned with a mix of historical and contemporary elements, reflecting the emperor's taste for both tradition and modernity. Franz Joseph and his wife, Empress Elisabeth, also known as Sisi, spent much of their time at Schönbrunn Palace, and it was here that many of the most significant events of their reign took place, including the signing of the Austro-Hungarian Compromise in 1867.

After the end of the Austro-Hungarian Empire in 1918, Schönbrunn Palace was turned into a museum and opened to the public. The palace and its gardens have been meticulously restored and preserved, allowing visitors to experience the opulence and grandeur of the Habsburg dynasty. Today, Schönbrunn Palace is a UNESCO World Heritage site and one of the most visited attractions in Vienna, attracting millions of visitors each year who come to admire its exquisite architecture, lavish interiors, and beautiful gardens.

Hofburg Palace

Hofburg Palace, located in Vienna, Austria, is one of the most significant historical buildings in the city, with a rich history dating back over seven centuries. The palace has been the center of power of the Habsburg dynasty, the ruling family of the Austrian Empire, for over six centuries.

The earliest parts of the Hofburg Palace date back to the 13th century when the castle was built for Duke Albrecht III. The castle was expanded in the 15th and 16th centuries, and during the reign of Emperor Charles VI in the early 18th century, the Hofburg Palace became the seat of the Habsburgs' power.

Over the centuries, the palace was expanded and remodeled numerous times, and it became the residence of some of the most influential and powerful figures in European history. Some of the most famous residents of the palace include Emperor Franz Joseph I and Empress Elisabeth, better known as Sisi, who ruled over the Austro-Hungarian Empire in the late 19th century.

During World War I, the palace was used as the headquarters of the Austrian army, and after the war, it became the residence of the newly established Austrian Republic's president. During World War II, the palace was severely damaged, and it was only after a long and costly renovation that it was restored to its former glory.

Today, the Hofburg Palace is a major tourist attraction and serves as the official residence of the President of Austria. The palace complex includes many buildings, including the Imperial Apartments, the Sisi Museum, and the Imperial Silver Collection.

Visitors can explore the palace's many rooms, which are decorated with lavish furnishings and works of art, and learn about the palace's history and its residents through interactive exhibits and guided tours. The palace is also home to several museums and galleries, including the Imperial Treasury, which houses the Habsburgs' priceless collection of crowns, jewels, and other treasures.

The Hofburg Palace is not only a symbol of the Habsburg dynasty's power and wealth but also a testament to Vienna's rich history and culture. It remains one of the most iconic landmarks in the city and an essential stop on any visitor's itinerary.

St. Stephen's Cathedral

St. Stephen's Cathedral, also known as Stephansdom, is a magnificent Gothic-style cathedral located in the heart of Vienna, Austria. The cathedral is one of the most iconic landmarks of Vienna and a popular tourist attraction, drawing millions of visitors every year.

The history of St. Stephen's Cathedral dates back to the 12th century when Duke Leopold V of Austria ordered the construction of a Romanesque church on the site where the cathedral stands today. However, the original church was destroyed by fire in 1258, and work began on a new Gothic-style cathedral in 1359 under the patronage of Rudolf IV, Duke of Austria.

The construction of the cathedral was a long and arduous process, taking over 70 years to complete. It was finally consecrated in 1433, although work on the cathedral continued for centuries. The cathedral was expanded in the 16th and 17th centuries with the addition of a new choir and a south tower.

One of the most significant events in the history of St. Stephen's Cathedral was the siege of Vienna by the Ottoman Empire in 1683. During the siege, the cathedral served as a military outpost and was severely damaged by Turkish artillery fire. However, the cathedral was rebuilt and restored to its former glory over the next few years.

The 18th century saw further renovations to the cathedral, including the construction of a new altar and the addition of a new north tower. The cathedral also played an important role in the cultural and intellectual life of Vienna during this time, with famous musicians such as Mozart and Haydn performing there.

During World War II, St. Stephen's Cathedral suffered significant damage from Allied bombing raids. However, the cathedral was restored once again after the war, and today, it remains one of the most important religious and cultural landmarks in Vienna.

Visitors to St. Stephen's Cathedral can marvel at its stunning Gothic architecture, which features intricate stone carvings, beautiful stained-glass windows, and a 137-meter-tall south tower that offers panoramic views of the city. Inside the cathedral, visitors can see the magnificent high altar, which is adorned with gold leaf and beautiful sculptures, as well as the tomb of Prince Eugene of Savoy.

St. Stephen's Cathedral is not only a place of worship but also a cultural and historical treasure that reflects the rich history and heritage of Vienna.

Belvedere Palace

Belvedere Palace is a complex of two palaces, Upper Belvedere and Lower Belvedere, located in Vienna, Austria. The palaces were built in the early 18th century by Prince Eugene of Savoy, a famous Austrian general, and served as his summer residence. The name Belvedere means "beautiful view" in Italian, and the palaces were constructed on a hilltop overlooking the city of Vienna.

Construction of the palaces began in 1714, and they were completed in 1723. The palaces were designed by the famous Baroque architect Johann Lucas von Hildebrandt, who also designed several other prominent buildings in Vienna, including the Hofburg Palace and St. Peter's Church.

The Upper Belvedere Palace was the main residence of Prince Eugene of Savoy and was used for formal events and receptions. It features a grand entrance hall, ballroom, and several salons, decorated with frescoes, stucco work, and marble. The centerpiece of the palace is the grand Marble Hall, which features an impressive ceiling fresco and is considered one of the most beautiful Baroque halls in the world.

The Lower Belvedere Palace was used as a private residence and features a more intimate atmosphere than the Upper Belvedere. It was also used for art exhibitions and houses a collection of Baroque art, including works by famous artists such as Peter Paul Rubens and Rembrandt van Rijn.

After Prince Eugene's death, the palace complex changed hands several times and was used for various purposes. In the 19th century, the palaces were used as a summer residence by the Habsburg family, and in the 20th century, they were used as a military hospital and as the headquarters of the Austrian State Treaty negotiations in 1955.

In 1908, the Austrian government acquired the palaces and began a restoration project to restore them to their former glory. Today, the Belvedere Palace complex is a popular tourist attraction and houses a museum that features a collection of Austrian art from the Middle Ages to the present day. The complex also includes extensive gardens, fountains, and sculptures, which are a popular destination for visitors to Vienna.

Kunsthistorisches Museum

Kunsthistorisches Museum, also known as the Museum of Fine Arts, is a famous art museum located in Vienna, Austria. The museum is home to an impressive collection of European art from the ancient world to the modern era, including works by famous artists such as Raphael, Caravaggio, Rembrandt, and Vermeer. The museum building itself is also a work of art, designed in the Neo-Renaissance style and featuring a grand marble staircase and ornate interiors.

The history of the Kunsthistorisches Museum dates back to the 16th century, when Emperor Rudolf II began collecting works of art from around Europe. He was particularly interested in collecting pieces from the Italian Renaissance, and he assembled a vast collection of paintings, sculptures, and decorative arts. His collection became one of the largest and most important in Europe at the time.

After Rudolf's death, his collection was passed down to subsequent Habsburg rulers, who continued to add to it over the centuries. The Habsburgs were passionate collectors of art, and they spared no expense in acquiring new works. They also commissioned numerous portraits of themselves, which can be seen in the museum's collection today.

In the 19th century, Emperor Franz Joseph I decided to create a new museum to house the Habsburgs' extensive art collection. He chose the location of the former imperial palace on Ringstraße, and commissioned architects Gottfried Semper and Karl von Hasenauer to design the new building. The museum was completed in 1891, and it quickly became one of the most popular attractions in Vienna.

During World War II, the Kunsthistorisches Museum suffered extensive damage from bombing raids. Many of the works of art had to be moved to safe locations to avoid being destroyed. After the war, the museum was rebuilt and restored to its former glory.

Today, the Kunsthistorisches Museum is one of the most important art museums in the world, attracting visitors from all over the globe. Its collection includes over 4,000 paintings, as well as numerous sculptures, decorative arts, and historical artifacts. The museum also hosts temporary exhibitions throughout the year, showcasing works from other museums and private collections.

Visitors to the Kunsthistorisches Museum can explore the museum's vast collection at their own pace, or join one of the museum's guided tours to learn more about the history and significance of the works on display. The museum also offers educational programs for children and adults, as well as a range of special events throughout the year.

Overall, the Kunsthistorisches Museum is a must-visit destination for art lovers and history buffs alike. Its rich history, stunning architecture, and incredible collection of works make it one of the most impressive museums in the world.

Naschmarkt

Naschmarkt is a well-known market in Vienna, Austria, that has been in existence since the 16th century. This bustling market is a foodie's paradise and one of the most popular tourist attractions in the city. The name "Naschmarkt" comes from the German word "naschen," which means "to snack," indicating that the market has always been a place to find tasty treats.

The history of Naschmarkt dates back to the 16th century when it was established as a trading place for farmers and merchants to sell their goods. The market has undergone several changes over the centuries, but it has always been an essential part of Viennese culture and commerce. During the 19th century, the market began to expand, and more vendors started selling their wares. As a result, the city built permanent stalls and improved the infrastructure to accommodate the growing demand.

During World War II, the market suffered significant damage, and it was closed for several years for reconstruction. However, the market was reopened in 1949 and quickly regained its position as a center for food and culture in Vienna. Today, the Naschmarkt is one of the most popular places in the city for locals and tourists alike to shop, eat, and socialize.

Visitors to the Naschmarkt can find a wide variety of goods, including fresh fruits and vegetables, meat, cheese, bread, and pastries. There are also numerous stalls selling international cuisine, including Indian, Turkish, and Thai food. In addition to food, the market also has vendors selling clothing, accessories, and souvenirs.

One of the unique features of the Naschmarkt is its flea market, which takes place on Saturdays. Visitors can browse through vintage clothing, antiques, and other interesting items. The flea market is a great place to find unique gifts and souvenirs.

The Naschmarkt has become an important cultural hub in Vienna, with numerous events and festivals taking place throughout the year. The market is a great place to experience the local culture and cuisine, and visitors can easily spend an entire day exploring its stalls and sampling its many offerings.

In conclusion, the Naschmarkt is a vital part of Vienna's history and culture. Its long-standing tradition of providing quality food and goods to locals and visitors has made it a beloved attraction in the city. Its fascinating history and unique offerings make it a must-visit destination for anyone traveling to Vienna.

Vienna State Opera

Vienna State Opera, also known as Wiener Staatsoper, is one of the world's most renowned and esteemed opera houses. Located in the center of Vienna, Austria, the Vienna State Opera has been a hub of cultural and artistic excellence for more than a century.

The History of Vienna State Opera:

The idea of establishing an opera house in Vienna dates back to the early 18th century. However, it wasn't until the reign of Emperor Joseph II in the late 1700s that the first opera house was built in the city. Known as the Kärntnertortheater, the opera house was home to a number of notable performances, including Mozart's "The Marriage of Figaro."

In the early 19th century, the Kärntnertortheater was demolished, and a new opera house was commissioned by Emperor Franz Joseph I. The new opera house was designed by the renowned architect August Sicard von Sicardsburg and his partner Eduard van der Nüll, and construction began in 1861.

Unfortunately, tragedy struck during the construction of the new opera house. Eduard van der Nüll committed suicide, leaving Sicardsburg to complete the project on his own. Despite this setback, the Vienna State Opera was completed in 1869, and the inaugural performance took place on May 25th of that year.

Throughout the years, the Vienna State Opera has undergone several renovations and upgrades. In 1945, the opera house was severely damaged during World War II, and it took several years to repair and restore the building. In 1955, the Vienna State Opera reopened its doors to the public, and it has remained one of the world's most beloved opera houses ever since.

Architecture and Design:

The Vienna State Opera is a stunning example of neo-Renaissance architecture. The building features a grand façade adorned with columns, statues, and ornate decorations. The interior is just as impressive, with plush red velvet seats, elegant chandeliers, and intricate frescoes adorning the ceiling.

The stage of the Vienna State Opera is also a marvel of engineering and design. The stage is 18 meters wide and 24 meters deep, and it can accommodate even the most elaborate sets and productions. The opera house also boasts a state-of-the-art sound system, ensuring that every note and nuance of the music is heard clearly and crisply throughout the auditorium.

Performances:

The Vienna State Opera is renowned for its diverse and impressive repertoire. The opera house stages more than 300 performances each year, featuring some of the world's most talented singers, conductors, and musicians. The Vienna State Opera is particularly well-known for its productions of operas by composers such as Mozart, Strauss, and Wagner.

In addition to operas, the Vienna State Opera also stages ballets and other dance performances. The Vienna State Ballet is considered one of the finest in the world, and it regularly performs works by renowned choreographers such as Rudolf Nureyev and George Balanchine.

Conclusion:

The Vienna State Opera is a testament to the beauty and power of the performing arts. With its rich history, stunning architecture, and world-class performances, the Vienna State Opera remains one of the most beloved and prestigious opera houses in the world.

Prater Amusement Park

Prater Amusement Park, or simply known as Prater, is a popular tourist attraction located in the heart of Vienna, Austria. The park is known for its historic Ferris wheel, which has become an iconic symbol of Vienna's skyline, as well as for its many rides, games, and attractions.

The history of Prater dates back to the 12th century, when it was used as an imperial hunting ground by the Babenberg dynasty. It was not until 1766 that the area was opened to the public, when Emperor Joseph II declared it open to all Viennese citizens. In the following years, the park underwent several changes, with new attractions and entertainment options being added to the site.

One of the most notable additions to the park was the Riesenrad, or the Ferris wheel, which was built in 1897 to celebrate the Golden Jubilee of Emperor Franz Joseph I. The Ferris wheel was a technological marvel at the time, and its construction required the use of over 20,000 cubic meters of concrete and 430 tons of iron. The wheel stands at a height of 65 meters and has 15 gondolas, each of which can hold up to 30 people.

The Ferris wheel quickly became a popular attraction, and over the years, it has played host to many famous visitors, including the likes of Sigmund Freud, Orson Welles, and Graham Greene. Today, the Riesenrad remains one of the most popular attractions in Vienna, with thousands of visitors riding the wheel every day.

In addition to the Ferris wheel, Prater is home to a wide range of other rides and attractions. Visitors can ride roller coasters, bumper cars, and other thrill rides, or they can try their luck at one of the many games and stalls that are scattered throughout the park. There are also numerous food stalls and restaurants on site, serving up traditional Viennese dishes and international cuisine.

Over the years, Prater has undergone many changes and renovations, but it has always remained a beloved destination for locals and tourists alike. In 2004, the park underwent a major renovation, with many of the rides and attractions being modernized and updated.

Today, Prater remains one of the most popular tourist destinations in Vienna, attracting millions of visitors every year with its unique blend of history, entertainment, and fun.

Prater Amusement Park, also known as the Wiener Prater, is a popular public park and amusement park in Vienna, Austria. The park is home to a wide range of attractions including roller coasters, carnival games, a giant Ferris wheel, and much more.

The history of Prater dates back to the 16th century when the area was a hunting ground for the Austrian royal family. In the 18th century, Emperor Joseph II declared the area open to the public and the park became a popular destination for locals.

The park was officially opened as an amusement park in 1897 with the installation of the Riesenrad Ferris wheel. The Riesenrad, which stands 65 meters tall, quickly became an iconic symbol of Vienna and is still one of the park's most popular attractions today.

In the years that followed, Prater continued to expand with the addition of more rides, attractions, and games. During World War II, the park was heavily damaged by bombing and was left in a state of disrepair for several years.

In the 1950s, the city of Vienna invested in the restoration and redevelopment of Prater, bringing it back to its former glory. Today, the park attracts millions of visitors each year and is one of the most popular attractions in Vienna.

Some of the most popular attractions in Prater include the Riesenrad Ferris wheel, the Prater Tower, the Praterturm swing ride, the roller coasters, and the ghost train. The park is also home to several restaurants, cafes, and beer gardens where visitors can enjoy a meal or a drink while taking in the sights and sounds of the park.

Prater is open year-round and admission to the park is free. Visitors can purchase tickets for individual rides or buy an all-inclusive pass for unlimited access to all the park's attractions.

Overall, Prater Amusement Park is a must-visit destination for anyone traveling to Vienna, offering a unique mix of history, culture, and thrilling amusement park attractions.

Chapter 4

Culture and Arts

Vienna is a city that has always been deeply immersed in culture and the arts. From world-renowned classical music to fine art, architecture, and theater, Vienna is a cultural hub that has produced some of the most significant figures in the world of arts and culture. Here, we take a closer look at the city's rich cultural history and its contributions to the world of arts.

Music:

Vienna has a long-standing tradition in music, and it is often referred to as the "City of Music." It has been home to some of the most celebrated composers and musicians, including Wolfgang Amadeus Mozart, Ludwig van Beethoven, Franz Schubert, Johann Strauss, and Gustav Mahler. The city boasts a wealth of music venues, including the world-famous Vienna State Opera, which showcases the works of both Austrian and international composers. Additionally, the city is home to the Vienna Philharmonic Orchestra, which is considered one of the finest orchestras in the world, and the Vienna Boys' Choir, one of the most renowned choral groups.

Fine Art:

Vienna is also renowned for its contributions to the world of fine art. The city has been home to some of the most significant artists in history, including Gustav Klimt, Egon Schiele, and Friedensreich Hundertwasser. The city has numerous museums and galleries, including the Belvedere Palace Museum, which houses a collection of works by Klimt and Schiele, and the Kunsthistorisches Museum, which has an extensive collection of European paintings, sculptures, and decorative arts.

Architecture:

Vienna is home to a vast array of architectural styles, from Gothic and Baroque to Art Nouveau and contemporary designs. The city's historic center is a UNESCO World Heritage Site, and it boasts several iconic landmarks, including St. Stephen's Cathedral, the Hofburg Palace, and the Schönbrunn Palace. Vienna's Art Nouveau architecture is particularly noteworthy, with notable examples including the Secession Building and the Hundertwasserhaus.

Theater:

Vienna has a rich theatrical history, with a long-standing tradition of producing plays and operas. The city is home to several theaters, including the Burgtheater, which is one of the most famous theaters in the German-speaking world. Other notable theaters include the Vienna Volkstheater and the Raimund Theater. The city also hosts the Vienna International Dance Festival, which showcases the best contemporary dance from around the world.

In conclusion, Vienna is a city that is deeply immersed in culture and the arts. Its rich cultural history has produced some of the most significant figures in music, fine art, architecture, and theater. Today, Vienna continues to be a vibrant cultural hub that attracts visitors from around the world, drawn to its world-class museums, galleries, music venues, and theaters.

Mozart's Vienna

Vienna, Austria is known for its rich cultural history and is considered the birthplace of classical music. One of the most prominent figures in the city's musical history is Wolfgang Amadeus Mozart. The city played a major role in Mozart's life, and his influence is still felt today in Vienna's music scene.

Mozart first came to Vienna in 1781, at the age of 25, hoping to establish himself as a composer and musician. He had already gained fame throughout Europe for his operas and other works, but he hoped that Vienna, the musical capital of Europe, would provide him with even greater opportunities.

Mozart was warmly welcomed in Vienna and quickly established himself as a popular composer and performer. He was appointed as a court composer by Emperor Joseph II, and his music was performed regularly at the imperial court and in public concerts throughout the city.

Mozart's time in Vienna was also marked by personal tragedy. He suffered from financial difficulties and health problems, and his relationship with the emperor became strained. Mozart's wife, Constanze, gave birth to six children, only two of whom survived infancy.

Despite these challenges, Mozart continued to compose some of his greatest works during his time in Vienna. He composed some of his most famous operas, including "The Marriage of Figaro," "Don Giovanni," and "The Magic Flute," as well as numerous symphonies, concertos, and chamber music.

Today, Mozart's legacy is still very much alive in Vienna. His music can be heard throughout the city, and there are several museums and monuments dedicated to his life and work. The Mozarthaus Vienna is a museum located in the house where Mozart lived from 1784 to 1787, and it features exhibits on his life and works. The Vienna State Opera also regularly performs Mozart's operas, and the annual Mozart Week festival is held in his honor.

In addition to Mozart, Vienna has been home to many other influential composers and artists throughout history. The Vienna Philharmonic Orchestra is considered one of the finest in the world, and the city is home to numerous museums and galleries showcasing works by artists such as Gustav Klimt and Egon Schiele.

Vienna's cultural history is still celebrated and cherished today, with the city continuing to be a hub of art, music, and culture. From the stunning architecture to the rich musical traditions, Vienna is a city that truly embodies the beauty and elegance of European culture.

Mozart's time in Vienna was marked by both success and struggle. He arrived in the city in 1781, at the age of 25, with his wife Constanze and his young son. Vienna was the center of the music world at the time, and Mozart was eager to establish himself there.

He quickly gained fame for his piano playing and his operas, which were performed at the prestigious Burgtheater. In his first year in Vienna, he composed four operas, including "The Abduction from the Seraglio," which was a major success.

Mozart's music was popular with both the aristocracy and the general public. He performed for the emperor, Joseph II, and his sister-in-law, Marie Antoinette, who was then the queen of France. He also gave concerts in public venues, which were attended by large crowds.

Despite his success, Mozart struggled with financial difficulties throughout his time in Vienna. He was never able to secure a permanent position at the court, and he often had to rely on commissions and concert fees to make ends meet. He was also known for his extravagant spending habits, which only added to his financial problems.

Mozart's time in Vienna came to a tragic end. In the summer of 1791, he fell ill and was unable to work. He died on December 5 of that year, at the age of 35. His death was a great loss to the music world, and he was mourned by his fans and fellow musicians.

Today, Mozart's legacy lives on in Vienna. His music is still performed regularly at the Vienna State Opera and other venues around the city. Visitors can also explore the Mozarthaus Vienna, which was Mozart's home from 1784 to 1787. The museum contains exhibits about Mozart's life and music, as well as his original manuscripts and letters..

Vienna Philharmonic Orchestra

Vienna Philharmonic Orchestra is one of the most renowned orchestras in the world, known for its exceptional sound quality and the breathtaking performances that it delivers. The orchestra has a rich history that dates back over 175 years and has played a significant role in the development of classical music in Europe and the rest of the world.

The Vienna Philharmonic Orchestra was founded in 1842 by Otto Nicolai, who was a conductor and composer from Germany. The orchestra was created as a private organization, which meant that its members were responsible for its finances and management. This structure allowed the orchestra to be independent and focus on its artistic pursuits without having to worry about commercial considerations.

Over the years, the Vienna Philharmonic Orchestra has attracted some of the best musicians in the world, who have helped to shape its unique sound and reputation. Many of the members of the orchestra come from musical families and have been playing their instruments since childhood. This level of skill and dedication is evident in the high quality of the orchestra's performances.

One of the most important periods in the history of the Vienna Philharmonic Orchestra was during the 19th century, when it played a significant role in the development of classical music. The orchestra worked closely with many of the leading composers of the time, including Johann Strauss II, Johannes Brahms, and Anton Bruckner. It was also instrumental in the creation of the Vienna New Year's Concert, which has become one of the most famous and highly anticipated concerts in the world.

In the 20th century, the Vienna Philharmonic Orchestra continued to play a crucial role in the development of classical music. The orchestra played an important part in the revival of interest in the music of Gustav Mahler, who was a conductor with the orchestra for several years. The orchestra also collaborated with many of the leading conductors of the time, including Leonard Bernstein, Herbert von Karajan, and Georg Solti.

Today, the Vienna Philharmonic Orchestra continues to be one of the most respected and prestigious orchestras in the world. The orchestra performs over 200 concerts each year, both in Vienna and on tour, and has a vast repertoire that includes works by some of the most important composers in history. The orchestra also continues to be involved in the creation and promotion of new music, ensuring that classical music remains a vital and relevant art form.

In addition to its musical accomplishments, the Vienna Philharmonic Orchestra has also made important contributions to the cultural life of Vienna and Austria. The orchestra is involved in a variety of educational and outreach programs, which aim to make classical music accessible to everyone, regardless of their background or experience. The orchestra also supports the preservation and promotion of Viennese musical traditions, including the music of Johann Strauss II and the Viennese waltz.

Overall, the Vienna Philharmonic Orchestra is an institution that has played a vital role in the development and promotion of classical music for over 175 years. Its rich history, unparalleled musicianship, and commitment to excellence continue to make it one of the most important and beloved orchestras in the world.

Vienna Boys' Choir

Vienna Boys' Choir is one of the oldest and most renowned choirs in the world. Founded more than 500 years ago in Vienna, Austria, this choir has a rich history and has become a symbol of Austrian music and culture.

The Vienna Boys' Choir, also known as Wiener Sängerknaben in German, was founded in 1498 by Emperor Maximilian I, who wanted a choir for his court chapel. The choir was made up of 12 boys and their choirmaster, and they were known for their beautiful singing and musical talent. Over the years, the choir grew in popularity and began to perform at various events and venues around Vienna, including the Hofburg Palace and the St. Stephen's Cathedral.

Throughout the centuries, the Vienna Boys' Choir has had many famous composers write music specifically for them, including Mozart, Haydn, and Schubert. The choir has also performed for many famous figures in history, such as Napoleon Bonaparte and Queen Victoria. In fact, the choir's reputation became so widespread that by the 19th century, it was considered to be one of the most prestigious choirs in Europe.

During World War II, the Vienna Boys' Choir faced many challenges. Many of the boys were drafted into the army or sent away to boarding schools to escape the war, and the choir's home in Vienna was destroyed in bombing raids. However, despite these difficulties, the choir continued to perform and bring joy to audiences around the world.

Today, the Vienna Boys' Choir is still going strong, with a roster of around 100 boys between the ages of 10 and 14. The boys come from all over the world and are chosen based on their musical ability, as well as their academic and social skills. They live together in a boarding school in Vienna, where they receive a top-notch education while also training and performing as members of the choir.

The choir performs around 300 concerts each year, both in Vienna and on tour around the world. Their repertoire includes everything from classical pieces to pop songs, and their performances are known for their flawless harmonies and beautiful voices. The Vienna Boys'

Choir has also released many albums over the years, which have become beloved by fans all over the world.

In addition to their musical accomplishments, the Vienna Boys' Choir is also known for their charitable work. They frequently perform benefit concerts for various causes, such as disaster relief and children's charities. They also have a foundation that provides scholarships for young musicians and supports music education in schools.

Overall, the Vienna Boys' Choir is a cultural treasure that has stood the test of time. Their beautiful music and rich history have made them one of the most beloved choirs in the world, and their dedication to both music and charitable causes has earned them the admiration and respect of audiences around the globe.

Secession Building

The Secession Building, also known as the Vienna Secession, is a significant example of Viennese Art Nouveau architecture. It was built in 1898 as an exhibition hall for the Secessionist movement, a group of Austrian artists who sought to break away from the traditional artistic styles of their time.

The Secession Building was designed by the prominent Austrian architect Joseph Maria Olbrich, who was a member of the Secessionist movement himself. Olbrich designed the building to reflect the ideals of the movement, which sought to create a new style of art that was free from the constraints of tradition.

The building is located on Friedrichstraße, in the heart of Vienna, and features a distinctive dome made of gold leaf. The dome, which is often compared to a giant golden cabbage, has become an iconic symbol of Vienna's Art Nouveau architecture.

The Secession Building was not only a place for exhibiting the works of the Secessionists but also a platform for cultural and intellectual exchange. The building hosted numerous lectures, concerts, and exhibitions, featuring not only the works of the Secessionists but also those of other avant-garde artists from around the world.

One of the most famous exhibitions held at the Secession Building was the 14th Secessionist Exhibition in 1902, which featured the works of Gustav Klimt, one of the most renowned artists of the movement. Klimt's masterpiece, the Beethoven Frieze, was created specifically for this exhibition and is now considered one of the most important works of Viennese Art Nouveau.

The Secession Building continues to play an important role in Vienna's cultural scene today. It is home to the Association of Visual Artists of Austria, which was founded by the Secessionists, and hosts regular exhibitions and events.

In addition to its cultural significance, the Secession Building is also notable for its architectural innovations. Olbrich's use of modern materials and techniques, such as reinforced concrete and electric lighting, made the building a pioneering example of modern architecture.

Today, the Secession Building is recognized as one of the most important examples of Viennese Art Nouveau architecture and is a popular tourist attraction. Its distinctive golden dome and innovative design continue to inspire and influence artists and architects around the world.

MuseumsQuartier

MuseumsQuartier, also known as MQ, is one of the largest cultural complexes in the world, located in the heart of Vienna, Austria. It is a historic site that was once a royal court stables, but now is a cultural destination that includes over 70 cultural institutions, museums, galleries, performance spaces, and cafes.

History:

The MuseumsQuartier's history dates back to the 18th century when the Habsburg monarchy had a need for a large building to house the imperial court stables. It was designed by the architect Jean-Nicolas Jadot de Ville-Issey, and construction began in 1725. The Baroque-style complex was completed in 1735, and it served as a royal court stables for more than two centuries.

In the late 20th century, the complex was in a state of disrepair, and the city of Vienna decided to turn it into a cultural destination. In 1998, the city launched an international architecture competition to redesign the complex, and the winners were architects Laurids and Manfred Ortner. They developed a plan to transform the former imperial court stables into a modern cultural complex.

After years of renovation and restoration, the MuseumsQuartier opened its doors in 2001. It quickly became a popular cultural destination in Vienna, attracting locals and tourists alike.

Attractions:

The MuseumsQuartier houses a wide range of cultural institutions, including art galleries, museums, performance spaces, and restaurants. Some of the most popular attractions include the Leopold Museum, the MUMOK (Museum of Modern Art), the Kunsthalle Wien, and the Architekturzentrum Wien.

The Leopold Museum is home to one of the largest collections of modern Austrian art in the world. It features works by artists such as Gustav Klimt, Egon Schiele, and Oskar Kokoschka. The MUMOK, on the other hand, has a large collection of modern and contemporary art, with works by artists such as Andy Warhol, Roy Lichtenstein, and Pablo Picasso.

In addition to the museums, the MuseumsQuartier has several performance spaces, including the Tanzquartier Wien, which hosts contemporary dance performances, and the Volkstheater, which stages plays and other performances.

Visitors can also relax and enjoy the atmosphere at one of the many cafes and restaurants in the complex. The MuseumsQuartier has several outdoor seating areas, making it a popular spot for people-watching and socializing.

Conclusion:

The MuseumsQuartier is a must-visit destination for anyone interested in culture and the arts. With its wide range of museums, galleries, performance spaces, and cafes, it offers something for everyone. It is a testament to the city of Vienna's commitment to preserving its cultural heritage and transforming it into a modern and vibrant destination.

Vienna State Opera

The Vienna State Opera, or Wiener Staatsoper in German, is one of the world's most prestigious and renowned opera houses. Located in the heart of Vienna, Austria, it is a cultural landmark that has been entertaining audiences for over 150 years.

The origins of the Vienna State Opera date back to the 1700s when Emperor Charles VI commissioned the construction of the Court Opera House. This first opera house was completed in 1724 and was later renamed the Kärntnertor Theater. Despite being an important venue for performances, the building was too small to accommodate the growing audience, and the need for a larger venue became apparent.

In the mid-1800s, Emperor Franz Joseph I commissioned the construction of a new opera house, which was completed in 1869. The new building was designed by the architects August Sicard von Sicardsburg and Eduard van der Null in the Neo-Renaissance style. Tragically, Eduard van der Null committed suicide shortly after the construction began, leaving Sicardsburg to complete the project alone.

The new Vienna State Opera was a magnificent building with a grand façade, majestic staircases, and opulent interiors decorated with marble, gold leaf, and crystal chandeliers. It quickly became a symbol of the city's rich cultural heritage and an iconic landmark of Vienna.

The Vienna State Opera soon became one of the world's most important and prestigious opera houses, attracting the best singers, conductors, and composers of the time. Legendary conductors such as Gustav Mahler and Herbert von Karajan, and famous composers such as Richard Strauss and Giacomo Puccini, all had their works premiered at the Vienna State Opera.

Over the years, the Vienna State Opera has undergone several renovations and refurbishments to maintain its splendor and modernize its facilities. The most significant renovation took place in the 1950s after the building suffered extensive damage during World War II. The restoration work was completed in 1955, and the Vienna State Opera reopened its doors to the public, with a performance of Beethoven's Fidelio.

Today, the Vienna State Opera is one of the busiest and most prestigious opera houses in the world, with over 300 performances annually. It has a seating capacity of 2,284, and its repertoire includes over 50 operas and ballets, from the classics of Mozart, Verdi, and Wagner to contemporary works by modern composers.

In addition to its regular performances, the Vienna State Opera is also renowned for its annual Vienna Opera Ball, which takes place every February. The ball is a glamorous event that attracts guests from all over the world, with its stunning costumes, elegant décor, and the opportunity to dance the night away in the grand hall of the opera house.

The Vienna State Opera remains a symbol of Austria's rich cultural heritage, and it continues to play a significant role in promoting the country's music and arts to the world.

Vienna Festivals

Vienna is a city that is full of culture and history, and this is reflected in the many festivals that take place throughout the year. These festivals celebrate music, art, theater, film, and more. They attract visitors from all over the world and are an important part of Vienna's cultural identity.

One of the most famous festivals in Vienna is the Vienna Opera Ball, which takes place annually in the Vienna State Opera. This elegant event is a highlight of the Austrian social calendar and features performances by the Vienna Philharmonic, as well as ballroom dancing and traditional Austrian music.

Another well-known festival is the Wiener Festwochen, which takes place every spring. This festival celebrates contemporary art, music, and theater, and features performances by artists from all over the world.

The Vienna Jazz Festival is another popular event, which takes place in the summer. This festival brings together some of the best jazz musicians from around the world and features concerts in a variety of venues throughout the city.

The Vienna Film Festival is also a major event, attracting filmmakers and film enthusiasts from all over the world. The festival features screenings of new and classic films, as well as discussions and workshops with filmmakers and industry professionals.

Other festivals in Vienna include the Vienna Festival of Lights, which takes place in November and features illuminated buildings and landmarks throughout the city, and the Vienna Christmas Market, which is held in the weeks leading up to Christmas and features traditional holiday food, crafts, and music.

In addition to these larger festivals, there are many smaller events that take place throughout the year. These include concerts, art exhibitions, and theater performances, as well as festivals celebrating traditional Austrian culture, such as the Wiener Wiesn Fest, which celebrates the country's beer and wine culture.

Overall, Vienna's festivals are an important part of the city's cultural heritage, and they offer visitors a unique opportunity to experience the city's vibrant arts and cultural scene. Whether you are interested in music, art, theater, film, or simply experiencing the city's unique cultural identity, there is something for everyone at one of Vienna's many festivals.

Chapter 5

Food and Drink

Vienna, the capital of Austria, is known for its rich culinary heritage and diverse food scene. From traditional Viennese dishes to international cuisine, the city offers a wide range of food and drink options to suit every taste and preference.

Viennese cuisine is a blend of different cultural influences, including Hungarian, Czech, and Italian, among others. The city is famous for its hearty dishes, such as Wiener Schnitzel, Tafelspitz, Gulasch, and Kaiserschmarrn, among others. Wiener Schnitzel, a breaded and fried veal cutlet, is one of the most popular dishes in the city and can be found in almost every traditional Viennese restaurant. Tafelspitz, a boiled beef dish served with horseradish and potatoes, is another local favorite. Gulasch, a Hungarian-style stew made with beef, paprika, and onions, is also popular.

Aside from traditional Viennese cuisine, the city is also known for its coffee culture. Viennese coffee houses are an integral part of the city's culinary heritage and offer a unique dining experience. They are known for their elegant interiors, comfortable seating, and extensive menus that include various types of coffee, cakes, and pastries. Some of the famous coffee houses in the city include Café Central, Demel, and Café Sacher.

Vienna is also famous for its wine culture. The city is surrounded by vineyards, and its wine-making traditions date back centuries. Some of the famous wine regions in Austria include Wachau, Kamptal, and Burgenland. Local wines such as Grüner Veltliner, Riesling, and Zweigelt are popular among locals and tourists alike. Wine taverns or Heurigers, which are family-run businesses, offer a unique experience to visitors. These establishments offer locally-produced wines, traditional food, and live music.

In addition to traditional Viennese cuisine, the city also offers a wide range of international food options. There are several restaurants in the city that serve Italian, Spanish, Japanese, and Chinese cuisine, among others. The Naschmarkt, a popular open-air market in Vienna, is home to numerous food stalls and restaurants that offer international cuisine. The market also sells fresh produce, spices, and herbs.

Overall, Vienna's food and drink scene is rich, diverse, and reflects the city's cultural heritage. From traditional Viennese dishes to international cuisine, visitors can experience a range of culinary delights in this vibrant city.

Traditional Viennese cuisine

Traditional Viennese cuisine is known for its rich flavors and hearty dishes that have been influenced by the city's location at the crossroads of different cultures. The cuisine of Vienna has its roots in the Habsburg Empire, which ruled over Austria and much of Europe from the 16th to the early 20th century. Over the centuries, Viennese cuisine has evolved to include a wide range of dishes that reflect the city's diverse culinary traditions.

One of the most famous Viennese dishes is Wiener Schnitzel, a breaded and fried veal cutlet that is typically served with a side of potato salad or parsley potatoes. Other popular dishes include Tafelspitz, a boiled beef dish that is often served with horseradish and apple-horseradish sauce, and Gulasch, a hearty stew made with beef, onions, and paprika.

Viennese cuisine also includes a variety of pastries and desserts that are renowned around the world. Perhaps the most famous of these is the Sachertorte, a rich chocolate cake filled with apricot jam and topped with a layer of chocolate icing. Other popular desserts include Apfelstrudel, a flaky pastry filled with apples and cinnamon, and Kaiserschmarrn, a fluffy shredded pancake served with fruit compote.

In addition to its traditional cuisine, Vienna is also home to a vibrant coffeehouse culture that dates back centuries. Coffeehouses have long been an important social hub in the city, where people gather to read, write, and discuss politics and culture over a cup of coffee or a slice of cake. Some of the most famous coffeehouses in Vienna include Café Central, Café Landtmann, and Café Hawelka.

Along with coffee, Vienna is also famous for its wine. The city is located at the center of Austria's wine-growing region, and many local vineyards produce excellent white wines, such as

Grüner Veltliner and Riesling. Viennese wine taverns, known as Heurigers, are popular destinations for locals and visitors alike, offering a chance to sample some of the region's best wines along with hearty traditional fare.

Overall, Viennese cuisine offers a unique blend of traditional and modern flavors that reflects the city's diverse cultural heritage. Whether you're looking to enjoy a classic Wiener Schnitzel or sample some of the city's famous pastries and wines, Vienna offers a rich culinary experience that is not to be missed.

Here are some additional details about traditional Viennese cuisine:

Wiener Schnitzel: This is perhaps the most famous Viennese dish, consisting of a thin, breaded and pan-fried veal cutlet. It is typically served with a side of potato salad or lingonberry jam.

Tafelspitz: This is a boiled beef dish served with a variety of traditional sides, including boiled potatoes, creamed spinach, and horseradish sauce.

Goulash: A hearty beef stew with onions, paprika, and other seasonings. It is typically served with a side of bread or dumplings.

Apfelstrudel: A classic Viennese dessert made with thin layers of pastry dough and filled with warm, spiced apples.

Sachertorte: A rich chocolate cake filled with apricot jam and topped with a layer of chocolate icing.

Kaiserschmarrn: A fluffy pancake made with eggs, flour, and milk, and served with a variety of toppings, such as fruit compote or caramel sauce.

Palatschinken: Similar to a crepe, palatschinken is a thin, rolled-up pancake filled with sweet or savory ingredients, such as fruit or cheese.

Wiener Würstel: A type of sausage that is a staple of Viennese street food. It is typically served with mustard and a side of bread.

Kärntner Kasnudeln: These are traditional pasta dumplings filled with a mixture of cheese, potato, and herbs. They are typically served with a side of butter or sour cream.

Erdäpfelgulasch: A vegetarian version of goulash, made with potatoes instead of beef. It is typically served with a side of bread or dumplings.

Overall, traditional Viennese cuisine is hearty, flavorful, and deeply rooted in the city's history and culture. Visitors to Vienna should not miss the opportunity to try some of these classic dishes during their stay.

Another popular dish is Tafelspitz, which is boiled beef served with potatoes, spinach, and horseradish sauce. This dish is considered a classic Viennese dish and is often served in upscale restaurants. It was said to have been a favorite of Emperor Franz Joseph I.

Another dish that is commonly found in Viennese cuisine is Gulasch, which is a beef stew with paprika and onions. It is often served with Spätzle, a type of egg noodle, or Knödel, a dumpling made from potatoes or bread.

Austrian desserts are also famous, and no trip to Vienna would be complete without trying some of these sweet treats. Sachertorte, a dense chocolate cake with a layer of apricot jam, is perhaps the most famous Viennese dessert. Other popular desserts include Apfelstrudel, a warm apple pastry served with vanilla ice cream, and Kaiserschmarrn, a shredded pancake served with fruit compote.

Viennese coffee houses are an integral part of the city's culinary culture. They have been around for centuries and were once gathering places for writers, artists, and intellectuals. Today, they are still popular places to enjoy a cup of coffee and some cake or pastries. Some of the most famous coffee houses in Vienna include Café Central, Demel, and Café Sacher.

In addition to coffee houses, Vienna is also known for its wine. The city is surrounded by vineyards, and there are many wine taverns, or Heurigen, where locals and visitors can sample local wines and traditional dishes.

Overall, traditional Viennese cuisine is a mix of hearty meat dishes, rich desserts, and strong coffee. It is a cuisine that is deeply rooted in the city's history and culture and has become an integral part of the Viennese way of life.

Viennese coffee culture

Vienna is renowned for its coffee culture, and the city has a long history of coffeehouses. Viennese coffee culture is a way of life, and the coffeehouses are the heart of the city's social scene. The coffeehouses in Vienna are not just places to have a coffee; they are places to relax, read the newspaper, meet friends, and even work. In this article, we will explore the history and culture of Viennese coffee and the coffeehouses that are so essential to the city's character.

History

Viennese coffee culture has a long history that dates back to the 17th century. According to legend, the first coffeehouse in Vienna, the Kaffeehaus zum Arabischen Coffe Baum, was opened in 1683 by an Armenian named Johannes Theodat. The coffeehouse was located in the Schlossgasse in the old city center and quickly became a popular meeting place for the city's intellectuals and artists.

In the following centuries, more and more coffeehouses were opened in Vienna, and they became a vital part of the city's culture. In the 19th century, the coffeehouses became even more important as they were places for political discussions and debates. Famous writers, artists, and intellectuals such as Franz Kafka, Arthur Schnitzler, and Gustav Klimt frequented the coffeehouses, and many of them wrote or sketched there.

Culture

The Viennese coffeehouse culture is not just about the coffee; it is about the experience. The coffeehouses in Vienna are designed to be comfortable and inviting, with plush chairs and sofas, marble-topped tables, and chandeliers. They are places to linger and relax, and the atmosphere is always lively and social.

In addition to coffee, the coffeehouses also serve a variety of snacks and pastries, such as the famous Sachertorte, a chocolate cake filled with apricot jam. Other popular pastries include Apfelstrudel, a pastry filled with apples and cinnamon, and Kaiserschmarrn, a sweet pancake topped with powdered sugar and served with fruit compote.

One of the most unique features of Viennese coffee culture is the way the coffee is served. Unlike in other parts of the world, where coffee is typically served in to-go cups, in Vienna, coffee is always served in a cup and saucer, with a small glass of water on the side. The water is meant to be sipped between sips of coffee to cleanse the palate.

Types of Coffee

Vienna has its own unique coffee culture, and there are several types of coffee that are famous in the city. Here are some of the most popular:

Melange - This is the most popular type of coffee in Vienna. It is similar to a cappuccino but has less foam and more coffee. It is made with espresso, steamed milk, and a dollop of froth on top.

Einspänner - This is a strong black coffee served in a small glass with whipped cream on top.

Fiaker - This is a coffee made with a shot of rum and whipped cream on top.

Kleiner Brauner - This is a small black coffee served with a small pitcher of milk on the side.

Conclusion

Viennese coffee culture is an essential part of the city's character and a beloved tradition. The coffeehouses in Vienna are not just places to have a coffee; they are places to relax, socialize, and be a part of the city's vibrant culture. If you are ever in Vienna, be sure to visit one of the city's many coffeehouses and experience the unique culture of Viennese coffee for yourself.

Wine taverns

Vienna has a long history of wine production, with vineyards located just outside the city limits In the 19th century, the city began to develop wine taverns, known as heurigers, as a way to promote local wine and provide a gathering place for people to enjoy it. Today, these wine taverns continue to be popular destinations for locals and visitors alike.

Heurigers are typically located in the vineyard areas on the outskirts of the city, such as Grinzing, Neustift am Walde, and Stammersdorf. They offer a casual, convivial atmosphere where guests can enjoy local wines by the glass or bottle, along with hearty Austrian fare.

One of the defining features of heurigers is their self-service model. Guests can simply grab a bottle of wine from a cooler or barrel, and pay for it at the end of the evening. The food is also self-serve, with a selection of cold cuts, cheeses, and hearty dishes like goulash and schnitzel available for guests to help themselves.

In addition to the food and wine, heurigers also offer live music, typically featuring local folk and jazz musicians. During the summer months, many heurigers have outdoor seating areas, where guests can enjoy the warm weather and scenic views of the vineyards.

Heurigers are open seasonally, typically from April to November, when the new wine is being served. Some heurigers also have their own wine shops, where visitors can purchase bottles to take home.

Overall, Vienna's wine taverns offer a unique and authentic way to experience the city's wine culture, and are a must-visit for anyone interested in local cuisine and wine.

Wine taverns, known as Heurigers in German, are a popular part of Vienna's culinary scene. These cozy, rustic establishments serve wine produced by local vineyards, along with traditional Viennese dishes.

Vienna has a long history of wine production, with vineyards located in the city's outskirts. Many of these vineyards are family-owned and operated, and the wine produced there is only available in local wine taverns.

Traditionally, wine taverns were only allowed to serve their own wine, which is why they are sometimes referred to as Buschenschanken (literally "bush taverns"). However, in recent years, some wine taverns have been granted a wider selection of wines to offer their customers.

The atmosphere in a typical Viennese wine tavern is relaxed and informal, with wooden tables and chairs, and a cozy, rustic decor. Guests can sit inside or outside, weather permitting, and enjoy a glass of wine alongside a hearty meal.

In addition to wine, wine taverns serve traditional Viennese cuisine, such as schnitzel, sausages, and goulash, as well as lighter fare like cheese and charcuterie plates. Many wine taverns also have live music, often featuring local musicians playing traditional Viennese folk music.

One unique aspect of Viennese wine taverns is their "open door" policy. Instead of a traditional storefront, wine taverns often have a small wooden sign hanging outside, indicating that they are open for business. Guests are welcome to come in and enjoy a glass of wine or a meal, even if they don't know the owner or have a reservation.

Overall, Viennese wine taverns are a beloved part of the city's cultural heritage, and are a must-visit for any food and wine lover visiting Vienna.

Vienna's wine taverns, also known as Heuriger, are a unique and cherished part of the city's culinary culture. These traditional establishments offer visitors the opportunity to sample locally-produced wines and enjoy hearty, rustic cuisine in a convivial atmosphere.

The history of Viennese wine taverns dates back to the 18th century, when the Emperor Joseph II granted winemakers the right to sell their own wine and food without a license. This allowed small-scale winemakers to sell their own products directly to the public, and the tradition of the Heuriger was born.

Initially, these establishments were little more than makeshift stalls set up in the vineyards themselves, where farmers could sell their wine and offer refreshments to passing customers. Over time, however, the Heuriger evolved into more permanent structures, with cozy indoor spaces and outdoor seating areas.

Today, Heuriger can be found in various districts around Vienna, particularly in the outlying areas of Grinzing, Neustift, and Stammersdorf. These districts are home to the city's most picturesque vineyards, and offer visitors the chance to explore the beautiful countryside around Vienna while sampling some of the region's finest wines.

The wines served in Heuriger are typically young, fresh, and unpretentious, with a focus on the local grape varieties such as Grüner Veltliner, Zweigelt, and Blaufränkisch. Visitors can sample a variety of different wines by the glass or bottle, often accompanied by traditional Viennese dishes such as Wiener Schnitzel, Tafelspitz, and Liptauer cheese spread.

In addition to their food and wine offerings, Heuriger are known for their convivial atmosphere and live music. Many establishments feature local musicians playing traditional Viennese music, creating a festive and relaxed atmosphere that is perfect for socializing with friends and family.

One of the unique features of Heuriger is the "Buschenschank" system. This allows small-scale winemakers to sell their own wines and products for a limited time period each year, typically during the harvest season. These temporary Heuriger offer visitors a chance to experience the authentic rural charm of Viennese wine culture, while sampling some of the region's best wines.

Overall, Viennese wine taverns offer a unique and authentic glimpse into the city's culinary culture, history, and traditions. Whether you are a wine lover, foodie, or simply looking for a relaxed and convivial atmosphere, a visit to a Heuriger is an essential part of any trip to Vienna.

Local markets

Vienna is known for its rich culinary culture, and a visit to the city would be incomplete without exploring the local markets. The markets offer a glimpse into the daily life of the Viennese and showcase the diversity of the city's cuisine. From fresh produce to local delicacies, the markets have something to offer for every food lover.

Naschmarkt, located in the heart of the city, is one of the oldest and most famous markets in Vienna. The market dates back to the 16th century and has over 120 vendors selling a variety of products including fruits, vegetables, spices, cheese, meat, fish, and more. Naschmarkt is also known for its international food scene, with vendors selling dishes from all over the world. It's a great place to explore different cuisines and try new foods.

Another popular market is the Brunnenmarkt, located in the Ottakring district. The market is open all year round and offers a wide selection of fruits, vegetables, meat, and fish. Brunnenmarkt is also known for its affordable prices, making it a popular spot for locals and tourists alike. The market has a vibrant atmosphere and is a great place to immerse oneself in Viennese culture.

Karmelitermarkt, located in the Leopoldstadt district, is another popular market in Vienna. The market is known for its organic produce and has a wide range of vendors selling everything from fruits and vegetables to artisanal cheese and baked goods. Karmelitermarkt also has a great selection of street food vendors and is a great place to grab a quick bite to eat.

One of the newer markets in Vienna is the Yppenplatz market, located in the Ottakring district. The market is open on Saturdays and features vendors selling organic produce, fresh baked goods, artisanal cheese, and more. Yppenplatz is also known for its trendy and hipster vibe, making it a great spot for young people to hang out and grab a coffee or a bite to eat.

Lastly, the Rochusmarkt, located in the Landstraße district, is a smaller and more intimate market. The market has a great selection of local produce, meat, and fish, as well as specialty items such as truffles and caviar. Rochusmarkt is also known for its great selection of flowers and plants, making it a popular spot for gardeners and plant enthusiasts.

In conclusion, Vienna's local markets offer a unique and authentic look into the city's culinary culture. Whether you're looking to explore new cuisines, try local delicacies, or simply immerse yourself in Viennese culture, the markets have something to offer for everyone.

Chapter 7

Shopping

Vienna is a city known for its fashion, luxury goods, and design, making it a shopping paradise for locals and visitors alike. From famous international brands to traditional handicrafts, Vienna has something to offer for everyone.

One of the most famous shopping streets in Vienna is Mariahilfer Straße, located in the heart of the city. It is the largest and most popular shopping street in Vienna, with a wide range of stores and boutiques selling everything from clothing and shoes to accessories and home decor. Some of the biggest brands in the world, such as Zara, H&M, and Mango, have flagship stores on this street. The street is pedestrian-only and is bustling with activity, making it a great place to stroll and shop.

Another popular shopping destination is the Goldenes Quartier, a luxury shopping area in the first district of Vienna. This area is home to high-end international brands such as Prada, Louis Vuitton, and Chanel. The Goldenes Quartier also has several restaurants and cafes, making it a great place to take a break from shopping and grab a bite to eat.

Vienna is also famous for its markets, which offer a wide variety of goods and fresh produce. One of the most famous is the Naschmarkt, located in the 6th district of Vienna. The Naschmarkt is a large outdoor market that sells everything from fresh fruits and vegetables to meat, fish, and cheese. It is also a great place to find spices, teas, and traditional Viennese sweets. The market is open every day except Sunday and is a popular destination for both locals and tourists.

For those interested in traditional handicrafts and souvenirs, the city has several options. One of the most famous is the Augarten Porcelain Manufactory, which has been producing high-quality porcelain products for over 300 years. The manufactory offers guided tours, where visitors can see the porcelain being made and purchase products in the on-site shop.

Another traditional handicraft in Vienna is the production of dirndls and lederhosen. These traditional clothing items are often worn during festivals and special events in Austria and are available in many shops throughout the city. Visitors can also purchase traditional Austrian crafts such as hand-carved wooden toys, glassware, and ceramics.

Overall, Vienna is a fantastic destination for shopping, with something to offer for every taste and budget. From luxury goods to traditional handicrafts, the city's shopping options are as diverse as its culture and history.

Mariahilfer Strasse

Mariahilfer Strasse is the largest shopping street in Vienna, Austria, located in the 6th and 7th district of the city. The street stretches for 1.8 miles (2.9 km) and features over 170 stores, ranging from international chains to local boutiques, making it one of the most popular shopping destinations in the city.

The history of Mariahilfer Strasse dates back to the 17th century when it was known as a country road that connected the city of Vienna to the nearby town of Mariazell. It wasn't until the 19th century that the street became a major commercial center in Vienna, with the construction of several large department stores and shops.

Today, Mariahilfer Strasse is a bustling pedestrian street that attracts both locals and tourists. The street is divided into two sections: the western section, known as Mariahilfer Strasse, and the eastern section, known as Mariahilfer Strasse-Ecke Neubaugasse.

The western section of Mariahilfer Strasse features large department stores, such as Peek & Cloppenburg, H&M, Zara, and Mango, as well as local boutiques and shops. The street is also home to several shopping centers, including the Gerngross Shopping Center and the Mariahilfer Strasse Shopping Center, which offer a wide range of products and services.

The eastern section of Mariahilfer Strasse is known for its independent stores and boutiques, as well as its vibrant street market. The market is held every Thursday and Saturday and features a variety of vendors selling fresh produce, baked goods, and handmade crafts.

In addition to its shopping options, Mariahilfer Strasse is also home to several restaurants, cafes, and bars, making it a popular destination for both shopping and dining. The street has something for everyone, from fast food chains to high-end restaurants, and from traditional Viennese cafes to trendy bars.

Overall, Mariahilfer Strasse is a must-visit destination for anyone who loves shopping and wants to experience the vibrant atmosphere of Vienna's bustling shopping district. With its diverse range of stores, restaurants, and cafes, there's always something new to discover on this famous street.

Graben and Kohlmarkt

Graben and Kohlmarkt are two of the most famous shopping streets in Vienna, Austria. Located in the city center, they are lined with luxury shops, high-end boutiques, and some of Vienna's most historic landmarks.

Graben is a narrow, pedestrian-only street that runs from St. Stephen's Cathedral to the Hofburg Palace. The street is named after the trench that was dug here in the 12th century to defend the city from invaders. Today, it is a bustling shopping street, known for its elegant shops and cafes.

Kohlmarkt is a continuation of Graben, stretching from the Hofburg Palace to Michaelerplatz. The street is named after the coal that was sold here in the Middle Ages. Today, it is home to some of the most exclusive and expensive shops in Vienna, including luxury brands such as Chanel, Dior, and Louis Vuitton.

The two streets are connected by a number of narrow alleyways and courtyards, many of which are home to smaller shops and cafes. These hidden corners of the city are a favorite of locals and visitors alike, offering a quieter and more relaxed shopping experience.

One of the most famous landmarks on Graben is the Plague Column, a monument erected in the 17th century to commemorate the end of a plague outbreak. It features a statue of the Virgin Mary standing atop a column, surrounded by allegorical figures representing the virtues that helped the city overcome the disease.

Another notable landmark on Graben is the Haas Haus, a modernist building designed by Austrian architect Hans Hollein in the 1990s. The building's curved glass facade is a striking contrast to the Baroque and Gothic architecture of the surrounding buildings.

Kohlmarkt is known for its historic buildings, many of which date back to the 18th century. One of the most impressive is the Palais Ferstel, a grand Renaissance Revival building that was built in 1856. Today, it houses a variety of shops, cafes, and restaurants.

Another historic building on Kohlmarkt is the Demel Cafe, a famous Viennese cafe that has been serving coffee and pastries since the 18th century. The cafe is known for its elaborate cakes and pastries, as well as its traditional Viennese coffee culture.

In addition to luxury shops and historic landmarks, Graben and Kohlmarkt are also home to a number of street performers and musicians. On weekends and holidays, the streets are filled with people enjoying the lively atmosphere and browsing the many shops and cafes.

Overall, Graben and Kohlmarkt are must-see destinations for anyone visiting Vienna. Whether you are looking for high-end shopping, historic landmarks, or a taste of Viennese culture, these streets offer something for everyone.

Naschmarkt

Naschmarkt is Vienna's most popular and oldest market that offers a unique shopping experience. The market is situated in the 6th district of Vienna, and it is one of the most vibrant places to visit. It has been operating since the 16th century and has grown to become a vital part of Vienna's cultural and culinary heritage.

The word 'Naschmarkt' is derived from the German word 'naschen,' which means snacking or nibbling. It is not surprising since the market offers a wide range of food and drinks, including fresh fruits and vegetables, meat, fish, cheese, spices, and sweets. In addition, the market also sells other items such as clothing, flowers, and souvenirs.

History

The history of Naschmarkt can be traced back to the 16th century when it was established as a place for farmers to sell their produce. During this time, the market was not as organized as it is today. The farmers used to sell their goods from their horse-drawn carts, which they parked along the street. However, as the demand for fresh produce increased, the market started to take shape, and vendors began to build permanent stalls.

The market gained popularity in the 18th century when it became the official supplier of fresh produce to the Imperial Court. During this period, the market underwent significant renovations, and the permanent stalls were replaced with brick buildings that were built in the Art Nouveau style.

In the early 20th century, Naschmarkt became a melting pot of different cultures, as immigrants from Eastern Europe, Asia, and the Middle East started to set up shop in the market. This led to a diverse range of food and drinks being offered at the market.

Today, Naschmarkt is one of the most popular tourist destinations in Vienna. The market has been renovated and expanded over the years, and it now covers an area of 1.5 km. The market attracts both locals and tourists who come to experience the unique atmosphere and to sample the different foods and drinks on offer.

Shopping

Naschmarkt offers an unparalleled shopping experience, with over 120 stalls selling a variety of goods. The market is particularly famous for its fresh produce, including fruits, vegetables, meat, and fish. Visitors can find a wide range of exotic fruits and vegetables that are not commonly found in other parts of the world.

The market is also home to a wide range of specialty shops that sell items such as cheese, olives, spices, and exotic teas. Visitors can also find souvenirs, clothing, and household items at the market.

Food and Drink

One of the highlights of Naschmarkt is the food and drink. The market has numerous restaurants, cafes, and street food stalls that offer a wide range of dishes from different cultures. Visitors can sample traditional Austrian dishes, as well as exotic cuisines from countries such as Turkey, Greece, and Iran.

The market is particularly famous for its Viennese coffee culture, and there are numerous cafes where visitors can enjoy a cup of coffee and a slice of cake. The coffee culture at Naschmarkt is an essential part of Viennese tradition, and visitors can experience it in its purest form.

Conclusion

Naschmarkt is a must-visit destination for anyone who wants to experience the cultural and culinary heritage of Vienna. The market offers a unique shopping experience, with a wide range of goods on offer. Visitors can sample different foods and drinks from around the world and experience the Viennese coffee culture in its purest form. Naschmarkt is a vibrant and bustling lace that is full of life and energy, and it is sure to leave a lasting impression on anyone who isits.

Flea Markets

lea markets are a popular attraction for tourists and locals alike in many cities around the world, and Vienna is no exception. The city is home to several well-known flea markets that ffer a unique shopping experience, where visitors can find everything from antiques and intage items to handmade crafts and artisanal foods.

)ne of the most popular flea markets in Vienna is the Naschmarkt, which is held every aturday. Located in the 6th district of the city, the market offers a wide variety of goods ncluding fresh produce, meats, cheeses, and baked goods. In addition to food items, visitors an also find clothing, antiques, and collectibles.

Another popular flea market in Vienna is the Flohmarkt am Wienerberg. This market is located on the southern outskirts of the city and is open every Saturday and Sunday. Visitors can find a variety of goods here, including vintage clothing, records, books, and furniture.

or those interested in antiques and collectibles, the Antikmarkt am Hof is the place to go. ocated in the heart of Vienna's historic center, this market is open on Saturdays and offers a wide range of antique and vintage items, including furniture, jewelry, and artwork.

Vienna is also home to several smaller flea markets that are worth a visit. The Brunnenmarkt in he 16th district is a popular market that offers fresh produce, meats, and cheeses as well as clothing and accessories. The Karmelitermarkt in the 2nd district is another popular market that offers fresh produce, handmade crafts, and artisanal foods.

Whether you're a seasoned collector or simply looking for a unique shopping experience, Vienna's flea markets offer something for everyone. Visitors can enjoy browsing the stalls, haggling with vendors, and discovering hidden treasures that they won't find anywhere else. With its rich history and vibrant culture, Vienna's flea markets are a must-visit destination for anyone visiting the city.

Chapter 7

Day Trips from Vienna

Vienna is not only a stunning city full of history, culture, and charm, but it is also the perfect starting point for several exciting day trips. Here are some of the best options for day trips from Vienna:

Wachau Valley: Located just an hour's drive from Vienna, the Wachau Valley is a UNESCO World Heritage Site and a stunning area of natural beauty. The valley is dotted with picturesque towns and vineyards and is home to some of the best wine in Austria. Visitors can take a leisurely boat ride along the Danube River or explore the charming towns of Durnstein and Melk.

Salzburg: Known as the birthplace of Mozart, Salzburg is a beautiful city located around 3 hours away from Vienna by train. This picturesque city is full of Baroque architecture and stunning views of the Alps. Visitors can explore the city's charming old town, visit the famous Salzburg Cathedral, and take in the stunning views from the Hohensalzburg Fortress.

Bratislava: Located just an hour away from Vienna by boat, Bratislava is the capital of Slovakia and a charming city full of history and culture. Visitors can explore the city's charming old town, visit the famous Bratislava Castle, and enjoy the stunning views of the Danube River.

Budapest: Located around 2.5 hours away from Vienna by train, Budapest is the capital of Hungary and a city full of stunning architecture, thermal baths, and delicious food. Visitors can explore the famous Chain Bridge, visit the beautiful Hungarian Parliament Building, and relax in one of the city's many thermal baths.

Lake Neusiedl: Located just a short drive from Vienna, Lake Neusiedl is the largest lake in Austria and a popular spot for water sports and relaxation. Visitors can go sailing, windsurfing, or swimming in the lake, or explore the charming towns that surround it.

Graz: Located around 2.5 hours away from Vienna by train, Graz is the second-largest city in Austria and a charming city full of history and culture. Visitors can explore the city's charming old town, visit the famous Schlossberg Castle, and take in the stunning views of the city from the top of the Uhrturm tower.

Semmering Railway: The Semmering Railway is a UNESCO World Heritage Site and a stunning railway route that runs from Vienna to the town of Semmering. The route passes through the stunning Semmering Pass, which is known for its stunning views and beautiful scenery.

In conclusion, Vienna is the perfect base for exploring the stunning scenery, charming towns, and rich culture of Austria and its neighboring countries. Whether you're interested in history, architecture, food, or natural beauty, there is something for everyone in the surrounding areas of Vienna.

Wachau Valley

The Wachau Valley is a picturesque region located in the northeast of Austria, along the Danube River. The valley is famous for its beautiful landscape, historic architecture, and delicious wines. It is also recognized as a UNESCO World Heritage Site for its cultural significance and natural beauty.

The Wachau Valley is easily accessible from Vienna, and many visitors choose to take a day trip to explore the region. One of the most popular ways to explore the Wachau Valley is by taking a boat tour along the Danube River, which offers stunning views of the picturesque vineyards, quaint towns, and historic castles along the riverbanks.

Visitors can also take a scenic drive through the Wachau Valley, which is known for its winding roads and breathtaking views. The road takes visitors through small villages and vineyards, offering a glimpse of the traditional Austrian way of life.

The Wachau Valley is also known for its delicious wines, particularly the Grüner Veltliner and Riesling varieties. Visitors can visit local wineries to sample the wines and learn about the production process.

Another popular attraction in the Wachau Valley is the Melk Abbey, a stunning Benedictine monastery that dates back to the 11th century. The abbey is famous for its stunning baroque architecture, including the impressive library, which houses over 100,000 books.

Other attractions in the Wachau Valley include the town of Dürnstein, which is famous for its beautiful blue church tower, and the ruined castle of Aggstein, which offers stunning views of the surrounding valley.

Overall, the Wachau Valley is a must-visit destination for those interested in history, culture, and beautiful landscapes. With its charming towns, vineyards, and historic landmarks, it offers a unique glimpse into traditional Austrian life and is sure to leave a lasting impression on visitors.

Melk Abbey

Melk Abbey is one of the most famous landmarks in Austria and a UNESCO World Heritage Site. Located in the town of Melk, which is approximately 90 kilometers west of Vienna, it is a Benedictine abbey that sits atop a hill overlooking the Danube River.

The history of Melk Abbey dates back to the 11th century, when Leopold II, Margrave of Austria, donated the site to the Benedictine order. The abbey has undergone many changes over the centuries, with the current Baroque structure being built in the early 18th century.

The abbey is famous for its stunning architecture and design, with the highlight being the library. The library at Melk Abbey is one of the most beautiful in the world, and contains over 100,000 books, including many rare and valuable manuscripts. The ceiling of the library is adorned with frescoes depicting the four faculties of theology, philosophy, medicine, and law.

Another highlight of the abbey is the Imperial Staircase, a grand staircase that leads to the Emperor's Gallery. The staircase is adorned with statues and frescoes, and is considered one of the finest examples of Baroque design in the world.

Visitors to Melk Abbey can take guided tours of the abbey, which includes the library, the Imperial Staircase, the church, and the gardens. The gardens are also a popular attraction, with stunning views of the Danube River and the surrounding countryside.

In addition to its cultural and historical significance, Melk Abbey is also an important center of education and research. The abbey houses a gymnasium (high school) and a theological college, and is home to the International College of Benedictine Monks, where monks from all over the world come to study and live.

Overall, Melk Abbey is a must-see destination for anyone interested in history, culture, and architecture. Its stunning design and rich history make it one of the most important landmarks in Austria, and a true gem of the Baroque period.

Bratislava, Slovakia

Bratislava is the capital and largest city of Slovakia, located on the banks of the Danube River, just a short distance from Vienna. As one of the most accessible capital cities in Europe, Bratislava makes for a great day trip from Vienna or a weekend getaway.

History:

Bratislava has a long and fascinating history, having been inhabited by various peoples since prehistoric times. Over the centuries, it has been part of the Kingdom of Hungary, the Austrian Empire, Czechoslovakia, and since 1993, the independent Slovak Republic.

One of the most important landmarks in Bratislava is the Bratislava Castle, which dates back to the 9th century. It has been rebuilt and reconstructed many times over the years and today is an important symbol of Slovak national identity.

Things to Do:

There are many things to see and do in Bratislava, including:

Bratislava Castle: As mentioned above, the castle is an important landmark in the city and offers stunning views of the city and the Danube River.

Old Town: The historic Old Town of Bratislava is a beautiful area with narrow streets, colorful buildings, and many restaurants and cafes. It is also home to several important landmarks, such as St. Martin's Cathedral and the Old Town Hall.

Devin Castle: Located on a cliff above the Danube River, Devin Castle is a ruined fortress that dates back to the 9th century. It offers beautiful views of the surrounding area and is a popular spot for hiking and picnicking.

Danube River: The Danube River is a central part of life in Bratislava, with many boat tours and riverfront cafes and restaurants.

Slovak National Gallery: This museum houses a large collection of Slovak and Central European art, including works by many famous artists.

Food and Drink:

Slovak cuisine is hearty and comforting, with many dishes featuring meat, potatoes, and dumplings. Some popular dishes include:

Bryndzové Halušky: A traditional Slovak dish made with potato dumplings and a sheep cheese sauce.

Kapustnica: A hearty soup made with sauerkraut, sausage, and potatoes.

Živánska: A pork dish that is typically served with cabbage and dumplings.

Slovak beer: Slovakia has a growing craft beer scene, with many small breweries producing high-quality beers.

Transportation:

Bratislava is easily accessible from Vienna by train or bus, with journey times of around an hour Within the city, the public transportation system is efficient and easy to navigate, with buses, trams, and trolleybuses running regularly.

Conclusion:

Bratislava is a beautiful city with a rich history and culture, making it a great day trip or weekend getaway from Vienna. Whether you're interested in history, art, or just exploring a new city, there is plenty to see and do in Bratislava.

Salzburg

Salzburg is a city in western Austria, situated at the northern edge of the Alps. It is the fourth-largest city in Austria and the capital of the federal state of Salzburg. The city has a rich and fascinating history that dates back to the Neolithic period, but it is best known as the birthplace of Wolfgang Amadeus Mozart and the setting for the movie "The Sound of Music."

The earliest recorded history of Salzburg dates back to the Neolithic period, around 5,000 years ago, when the area was settled by the Celts. Later, the Romans established a settlement called Juvavum in the area, which grew into an important trading center due to its location on the River Salzach.

In the 7th century, the Bavarians took control of the region and established the Duchy of Bavaria. Salzburg became the seat of a bishop in the 8th century, and in the 11th century, it became a separate principality within the Holy Roman Empire. The city became a major center of trade and culture during this time, and many of its most important landmarks, such as the Hohensalzburg Fortress and the Salzburg Cathedral, were built.

In the 16th century, Salzburg became a center of the Counter-Reformation, a Catholic movement that aimed to combat the spread of Protestantism. The city's prince-archbishops, who were also the rulers of the region, embarked on a building spree to create grand churches and palaces that would demonstrate their power and influence.

During the 18th century, Salzburg experienced a period of cultural flourishing, particularly in the field of music. This was largely due to the presence of the Mozart family, who moved to the city in the 18th century and played an important role in its musical life. Wolfgang Amadeus Mozart was born in Salzburg in 1756, and he lived and worked there for much of his life. Many of his most famous works, including "The Magic Flute" and "Don Giovanni," were composed in Salzburg.

In the 19th and early 20th centuries, Salzburg underwent significant modernization, with the construction of new buildings and the expansion of the city's infrastructure. However, the city also suffered significant damage during World War II, with many of its historic buildings destroyed or damaged.

After the war, Salzburg underwent a period of reconstruction, and many of its most important landmarks were restored to their former glory. The city also became a major center of tourism, thanks to its rich cultural heritage and stunning natural surroundings.

Today, Salzburg is a vibrant and thriving city that combines its rich history with modern amenities and a lively cultural scene. It continues to attract visitors from all over the world, who come to explore its fascinating past and enjoy its many attractions and events.

Here are some reasons why Salzburg is a must-visit destination:

Cultural and historical significance: Salzburg is steeped in history and culture, with a rich artistic and musical heritage. It was the birthplace of Wolfgang Amadeus Mozart, and visitors can explore his former home and the places where he performed. The city is also home to the iconic Salzburg Festival, which celebrates music and the arts every summer.

Beautiful architecture: Salzburg's old town is a UNESCO World Heritage Site and is filled with stunning architecture from various periods, including Gothic, Baroque, and Rococo. Visitors can explore the city's many churches, palaces, and squares, including the iconic Mirabell Palace and Gardens and the Hohensalzburg Fortress.

Picturesque natural surroundings: Salzburg is surrounded by stunning Alpine scenery, including the nearby Untersberg mountain, which offers spectacular views of the city and its surroundings. Visitors can also take a stroll along the Salzach River or explore the nearby lakes and forests.

Unique culinary experiences: Salzburg is known for its culinary traditions, including the famous Salzburger Nockerln, a sweet soufflé-like dessert. Visitors can also try traditional Austrian dishes such as schnitzel, strudel, and dumplings, as well as locally brewed beer and Austrian wines.

Active pursuits: Salzburg offers visitors a range of outdoor activities, including hiking, skiing, and mountain biking in the surrounding mountains. Visitors can also take a leisurely bike ride along the Salzach River or enjoy a round of golf at one of the city's many courses.

Overall, Salzburg is a charming and picturesque city with a rich cultural heritage and stunning natural surroundings. It is an ideal destination for history and culture buffs, foodies, nature lovers, and adventure seekers alike.

Graz

Graz is a city in Austria with a rich and varied history that dates back to ancient times. The city has been inhabited for over 4,000 years and has been ruled by various empires and dynasties throughout its history. Today, Graz is a vibrant city known for its cultural and historical significance, as well as its stunning architecture and beautiful landscapes.

Graz was founded by the Celts in the 8th century BC, and was known as "Gradec" which means "small castle" in Slovenian. The city was strategically located on a hill overlooking the River Mur, which made it an ideal location for a castle. In the 12th century, the Babenberg family, who ruled over Austria at the time, built a fortress on the hill and made Graz their residence.

Over the next few centuries, Graz grew in importance and became a center for trade and commerce. In the 15th century, Graz became the capital of Styria, one of the provinces of Austria, and its importance continued to grow. The city's prosperity attracted merchants and artisans from all over Europe, and Graz became known for its textile industry and its skilled craftsmen.

During the Renaissance, Graz experienced a period of cultural and artistic growth. The city's rulers were patrons of the arts, and many beautiful buildings and works of art were created during this time. The most famous example of Renaissance architecture in Graz is the Landhaus, a beautiful palace that was built in the 16th century.

In the 17th and 18th centuries, Graz suffered from a series of disasters, including fires and plagues. However, the city was able to recover and rebuild, and many of the beautiful buildings and works of art that are still visible in Graz today date from this time.

In the 19th century, Graz became an important industrial center, and many factories were built in and around the city. This period of industrialization brought new wealth and prosperity to Graz, but it also had a negative impact on the city's environment and its quality of life.

After World War II, Graz began to rebuild and modernize, and today it is a vibrant city with a thriving cultural and artistic scene. The city is home to several universities and is known for its innovative and forward-thinking approach to urban planning and design.

Overall, Graz's history is a fascinating and complex story of growth, decline, and renewal. The city has been shaped by many different influences and forces over the centuries, and its rich cultural heritage is a testament to its enduring importance and significance. Today, visitors to Graz can explore the city's fascinating history through its many museums, historic buildings, and beautiful public spaces.

Here are some tips on how to make the most of your time in the city:

Explore the old town: Graz's old town is a UNESCO World Heritage Site and is home to many beautiful buildings and historic landmarks. Take a stroll through the narrow streets and alleys and admire the unique architecture, such as the Gothic-style Graz Cathedral, the Renaissance-era Landhaus, and the Baroque-style Eggenberg Palace.

Visit the museums: Graz has a wide range of museums that cater to all interests, from art to history to science. The Kunsthaus Graz is a modern art museum that showcases contemporary art from around the world, while the Landesmuseum Joanneum is the largest museum complex in Austria and features exhibits on art, history, and natural history.

Enjoy the food: Graz is known for its culinary scene and is home to many great restaurants and cafes. Be sure to try local specialties such as Styrian pumpkin seed oil, which is used in many dishes, and Styrian wine, which is produced in the surrounding region.

Take in the views: Graz is situated in a picturesque location, surrounded by hills and forests. Head to the Schlossberg, a hill in the city center, for panoramic views of the city and the surrounding countryside. You can take a funicular to the top or hike up for a more challenging experience.

Attend a festival: Graz hosts many festivals throughout the year, celebrating everything from music to food to cultural heritage. The Styriarte festival is a popular music festival that features classical and contemporary music performances, while the GenussHauptstadt Graz festival is a celebration of local food and wine.

Overall, Graz is a vibrant and exciting city that has a lot to offer visitors. Whether you're interested in history, culture, or food, there's something for everyone to enjoy.

Graz, the second-largest city in Austria, is a safe destination for visitors. The city is known for its low crime rate, and the local authorities have taken measures to ensure the safety of residents and tourists.

The city has a well-trained and equipped police force that is always ready to respond to emergencies. Graz police are easily recognizable by their green uniforms and can be found patrolling the streets and public places, ensuring the safety of the residents and visitors.

In addition, there are several safety measures in place to ensure the safety of visitors in public areas. CCTV cameras are installed in strategic locations, especially in busy areas like the train station, shopping malls, and other public places.

One of the most important things for visitors to note is that Graz is generally a safe place, but visitors should take necessary precautions to avoid becoming victims of crime. Visitors should always be aware of their surroundings and take care of their valuables, such as passports, money, and other important documents. It is important to keep these items in a safe place, such as a hotel safe or a money belt.

Visitors should also be cautious when using ATMs and avoid withdrawing large amounts of money. Instead, it is recommended to withdraw small amounts of cash as needed.

In addition, visitors should avoid walking alone at night, especially in areas that are not well-lit. It is recommended to use a taxi or public transportation when traveling at night.

Furthermore, it is essential to be cautious when interacting with strangers, especially those who offer unsolicited help or try to engage in conversation. Visitors should also be wary of scams, such as fake police officers or street vendors selling counterfeit goods.

Overall, visitors to Graz can enjoy a safe and secure experience as long as they take the necessary precautions to ensure their safety. The city's authorities are committed to maintaining a safe and welcoming environment for all visitors, and visitors can feel confident in their ability to enjoy all that Graz has to offer.

Chapter 8

Practical Information

Vienna, Austria is a vibrant and exciting city with a rich history, diverse culture, and countless things to do and see. To make the most of your visit, it's important to have some practical information about the city, including transportation, currency, language, and more.

Language:

The official language of Austria is German, but English is widely spoken, particularly in tourist areas. It's always helpful to learn a few basic phrases in German to help with communication.

Currency:

The currency in Austria is the Euro (EUR). ATMs are widely available throughout the city, and most shops, restaurants, and hotels accept credit cards. However, it's always a good idea to carry some cash with you for smaller purchases and for use at markets and street vendors.

Electricity:

The standard voltage in Austria is 230V, and the frequency is 50Hz. Plugs are typically Type C (Europlug) or Type F (Schuko).

Transportation:

Vienna has an excellent public transportation system, including buses, trams, and the U-Bahn (subway). Tickets can be purchased at ticket machines in U-Bahn stations or at many tobacco shops throughout the city. It's important to validate your ticket before boarding the bus or U-Bahn, as there are frequent ticket checks. Taxis are also readily available, but can be more expensive than public transportation.

Climate:

Vienna has a moderate continental climate, with warm summers and cold winters. The best time to visit is generally from April to October, when the weather is mild and there are many outdoor activities and events.

Safety:

Vienna is generally a very safe city, with low levels of crime. However, it's important to be aware of your surroundings, particularly in tourist areas where pickpocketing can occur. It's also important to be cautious when using public transportation late at night, and to avoid walking alone in unlit areas.

Emergency services:

In case of emergency, dial 112 for police, fire, or medical assistance.

Visa requirements:

Visitors from many countries, including the United States and most European countries, do not need a visa to visit Austria for stays of up to 90 days. However, it's always a good idea to check visa requirements for your specific country before traveling.

Overall, Vienna is a safe, exciting, and welcoming city with plenty to offer visitors. With a bit of preparation and practical information, you can make the most of your visit and have an unforgettable experience.

Emergency contacts

Emergency contacts are essential pieces of information that travelers should have at their fingertips while traveling abroad. In the event of an emergency, knowing whom to call and where to go for help can make a significant difference in the outcome. This is especially important when traveling to a foreign country where the language, customs, and healthcare system may differ from what you are accustomed to.

In Austria, the emergency number is 112, which will connect you to the European emergency number. This number can be used to contact the police, fire department, and ambulance services. It is important to note that emergency services in Austria may not speak English, so it is helpful to have a basic understanding of German or have access to a translation tool.

Medical emergencies can be handled through the ambulance services, which are operated by the Red Cross. They can be reached by dialing 144. If you need a doctor for a non-emergency situation, you can check with your hotel or the local tourist office for recommendations.

In the event of theft or loss of important documents such as passports or visas, you should contact your embassy or consulate. The US Embassy in Vienna can be reached at +43 1 313 390, and the UK Embassy in Vienna can be reached at +43 1 716 130.

It is also a good idea to keep a list of important phone numbers with you, including the contact information for your hotel or accommodations, tour operators, and any other relevant contacts. Additionally, if you have any health conditions or allergies, it is important to have this information readily available in case of an emergency.

Overall, while traveling in Austria, it is always better to be prepared for emergencies, no matter how unlikely they may seem. Having access to emergency contacts and relevant information can give you peace of mind and make your trip more enjoyable and stress-free.

Language and communication

Language and communication are essential aspects to consider when traveling to a foreign country. In Graz, the official language is German, and while English is widely spoken in tourist areas, it is always helpful to learn some basic German phrases.

If you are in need of translation or interpretation services, there are several options available in Graz. The city has translation agencies and language schools that provide services such as translation, interpreting, and language courses.

For emergency situations where language barriers may pose a problem, the city has a multilingual emergency call center. The number to dial is 112, and the operators speak German, English, French, Italian, and Hungarian.

It is also important to note that Austria uses the European Union's standard plug sockets, which are Type C, Type E, and Type F. Make sure to bring the necessary adapters if you plan on using electrical devices during your stay.

When it comes to communication, Wi-Fi is widely available in hotels, cafes, and restaurants throughout Graz. If you need to stay connected while on the go, there are several prepaid SIM card options available for purchase. The major providers are A1, Magenta, and Drei. These providers offer various data packages that can be purchased at their respective stores or through vending machines located throughout the city.

It is worth noting that while using mobile data, roaming charges may apply if you are traveling from outside the EU. If you plan on using mobile data extensively, it may be more cost-effective to purchase a local SIM card.

Overall, while the language may pose a challenge for some, there are plenty of resources available in Graz to help visitors communicate effectively and stay connected during their stay.

Safety tips

When traveling to a new place, it's important to prioritize your safety and take certain precautions to minimize potential risks. Here are some safety tips to keep in mind during your trip to any destination:

Research your destination: Before you even leave for your trip, take some time to research your destination. Learn about the local customs and laws, potential dangers, and areas to avoid. This can help you stay alert and aware of your surroundings once you arrive.

Keep your valuables safe: Keep your valuables such as your passport, cash, and credit cards in a safe place. Avoid carrying large amounts of cash and leave any unnecessary valuables at home. Consider using a money belt or locking your luggage.

Be aware of your surroundings: Stay alert and aware of your surroundings, especially in unfamiliar areas. Keep an eye out for any potential dangers, and try to avoid walking alone in poorly lit or isolated areas.

Avoid sharing too much information: Be cautious about sharing personal information with strangers, especially when it comes to your itinerary or travel plans. Avoid announcing your travel plans or sharing too much on social media.

Be cautious with public Wi-Fi: Public Wi-Fi can be convenient, but it's important to use it with caution. Avoid accessing sensitive information such as banking or personal accounts on public Wi-Fi, as it can be easily hacked.

Use common sense: Finally, use common sense when traveling. If something seems too good to be true, it probably is. Be wary of scams and always trust your instincts.

It's also a good idea to register your trip with your embassy or consulate before traveling. This will allow them to reach out to you in case of an emergency and provide you with important updates and information regarding your destination. With these safety tips in mind, you can enjoy your trip with peace of mind.

Tipping etiquette

Tipping etiquette varies widely from country to country, and it can be a source of confusion for travelers who are unfamiliar with local customs. In general, tipping in Austria is not as common as it is in some other countries, such as the United States. However, if you receive good service it is customary to leave a small tip to show your appreciation.

In restaurants, it is common to round up the bill or leave a few coins as a tip. This is usually done by leaving the money on the table after paying the bill, rather than handing it directly to the server. If you have received exceptional service or if you are dining in a more upscale restaurant, you may want to leave a larger tip of around 10% of the total bill.

Tipping for drinks at a bar is not expected, but it is common to round up the bill or leave a small amount of change. In hotels, it is customary to leave a small tip for the housekeeping staff, usually around 1-2 euros per day.

Tipping for taxi rides is not common in Austria, but it is acceptable to round up the fare or leave a small tip of 1-2 euros. Some taxi drivers may also round down the fare to the nearest euro, which is a common practice in Austria.

It is important to note that while tipping is appreciated in Austria, it is not expected. If you do not wish to leave a tip, it will not be considered rude or disrespectful. It is always a good idea to check with locals or ask for advice from your hotel or tour guide to ensure that you are following local customs and etiquette.

Useful phrases

If you're planning a trip to a foreign country, it's always a good idea to learn a few useful phrases in the local language. Not only will it make your travels easier and more enjoyable, but it's also a sign of respect for the local culture. Here are some useful phrases in German, which is the official language of Austria:

Guten Tag! (Good day!) - This is a polite greeting that can be used any time of day.

Entschuldigung. (Excuse me.) - Use this phrase to get someone's attention or to apologize.

Sprechen Sie Englisch? (Do you speak English?) - This can be helpful if you need to communicate with someone who doesn't speak German.

Ich verstehe nicht. (I don't understand.) - If you're having trouble following a conversation, use this phrase to let the other person know.

Wie viel kostet das? (How much does that cost?) - This is a useful phrase to use when shopping or dining out.

Wo ist die Toilette? (Where is the bathroom?) - This phrase can be a lifesaver in a new city or country.

Ich hätte gerne... (I would like...) - Use this phrase when ordering food or drinks.

Danke schön. (Thank you very much.) - Always a good phrase to know, and a way to show your appreciation.

Auf Wiedersehen! (Goodbye!) - A polite way to say goodbye to someone.

Prost! (Cheers!) - A fun phrase to use when you're enjoying a drink with friends.

In addition to these basic phrases, it's a good idea to learn some local customs and etiquette. For example, it's customary to greet people with a handshake in Austria, and to address people formally until you are invited to use their first name. It's also important to be punctual and respectful of others' time.

Overall, learning a few basic phrases in German can go a long way in making your trip to Austria more enjoyable and memorable. It shows that you are making an effort to understand and appreciate the local culture, and can lead to more meaningful interactions with locals.

Chapter 9

Final thoughts on Vienna

Vienna is a city that truly has something for everyone. From the stunning architecture and rich history to the vibrant culture and delicious food, there is never a dull moment in this magnificent city. Whether you are interested in exploring the city's numerous museums and art galleries, indulging in some of the world's best coffee and pastry, or simply strolling through the city's parks and gardens, Vienna offers an unforgettable experience that will stay with you for a lifetime.

One of the things that makes Vienna so special is its dedication to preserving its rich history and cultural heritage. The city is home to numerous historic sites, including the stunning Schönbrunn Palace and Hofburg Imperial Palace, both of which offer an inside look at the opulence and grandeur of the Habsburg monarchy. The city is also home to numerous museums and art galleries, including the world-renowned Kunsthistorisches Museum and the Belvedere Palace, which houses one of the largest collections of Gustav Klimt's works.

But Vienna is not just a city of the past – it is also a vibrant and dynamic cultural hub, with a thriving contemporary arts scene, world-class music venues, and a lively nightlife. The city is home to numerous theaters, including the famous Burgtheater, as well as countless galleries, performance spaces, and music venues. Whether you are looking for classical music, modern dance, or avant-garde theater, you will find it all in Vienna.

Of course, no visit to Vienna would be complete without indulging in some of the city's famous coffee and pastry. Vienna is home to some of the world's best coffeehouses, where you can savor a rich cup of coffee and a delicious slice of cake while enjoying the elegant surroundings. The city is also famous for its pastry, with delights such as Sachertorte, Apfelstrudel, and Linzer Torte all hailing from Vienna.

In terms of shopping, Vienna is a paradise for those looking for high-end fashion and luxury goods. The city is home to numerous designer boutiques, as well as a plethora of high-end department stores, including the famous Steffl Department Store on Kärntner Strasse. For those looking for a more unique shopping experience, the city's numerous markets offer everything from fresh produce to handmade crafts and vintage clothing.

When it comes to getting around, Vienna has an excellent public transportation system, with buses, trams, and trains crisscrossing the city. The city is also very walkable, with many of its top attractions located within easy walking distance of one another.

In terms of safety, Vienna is generally considered to be a very safe city, with a low crime rate and a strong police presence. However, as with any large city, it is important to take basic precautions, such as keeping an eye on your belongings and avoiding unlit or deserted areas at night.

In conclusion, Vienna is a truly magical city that offers something for everyone. With its rich history, vibrant culture, delicious food, and stunning architecture, it is no wonder that Vienna consistently ranks as one of the world's top tourist destinations. Whether you are visiting for a weekend or a longer stay, Vienna is sure to leave a lasting impression and a lifetime of memories.

Encouragement to visit the city again.

Vienna is a city that is impossible to explore in just one visit. Its rich history, stunning architecture, and vibrant culture make it an unforgettable destination that will leave you wanting more. Whether you have already visited the city or are planning your first trip, there is always something new and exciting to discover in Vienna.

One of the best reasons to return to Vienna is the city's ever-evolving cultural scene. Vienna is known for its world-class music and theater, and the city hosts a variety of festivals and events throughout the year that showcase the best of the arts. Whether you are interested in classical music, opera, or contemporary art, Vienna has something for everyone.

Another reason to visit Vienna again is to explore the city's hidden gems. Despite being a major tourist destination, Vienna is full of lesser-known neighborhoods, museums, and attractions that are just waiting to be discovered. From the historic Jewish Quarter to the stunning Belvedere Palace, there is always something new to explore in Vienna.

If you have already visited the city's major tourist attractions, returning to Vienna will give you the opportunity to explore the city in a more relaxed and authentic way. Instead of rushing from one landmark to another, you can take your time to stroll through Vienna's charming streets, stop in local coffee shops, and soak up the city's unique atmosphere.

Finally, Vienna's food and drink scene is a reason in itself to return to the city. From traditional Viennese cuisine to international cuisine, Vienna's dining scene is as diverse as it is delicious. You can sample local delicacies at traditional coffeehouses, grab a quick bite from a street vendor, or enjoy a gourmet meal at a Michelin-starred restaurant.

In conclusion, Vienna is a city that offers something for everyone and is impossible to explore in just one visit. Whether you are interested in history, art, music, or food, Vienna will captivate you with its beauty and charm. So, why not start planning your next trip to Vienna today? You won't regret it!

Printed in Great Britain
by Amazon

23181535R00066